WOUNDS ARE WHERE
LIGHT ENTERS

ALSO BY WALTER WANGERIN JR.

# WOUNDS ARE WHERE LIGHT ENTERS

STORIES OF GOD'S INTRUSIVE GRACE

BY WALTER WANGERIN JR.

ZONDERVAN

*Wounds Are Where Light Enters*
Copyright © 2017 by Walter Wangerin Jr.

Requests for information should be addressed to:
Zondervan, *3900 Sparks Dr. SE, Grand Rapids, Michigan 49546*

ISBN 978-0-310-24005-1 (hardcover)

ISBN 978-0-310-35034-7 (ebook)

The author is represented by Alive Literary Agency, 7680 Goddard Street, Suite 200, Colorado Springs, Colorado 80920, www.aliveliterary.com

*Art direction: Curt Diepenhorst*
*Interior design and artwork: Denise Froehlich*
*Editorial team: John Sloan, Gwyneth Findlay, and Robert Hudson*

First printing September 2017 / Printed in the United States of America

*For Robert Hudson,*
*editor and friend*

# CONTENTS

## FIVE: IT'S THE LITTLE THINGS

## SIX: CATCHING THIEVES

## SEVEN: SERVING THE LEAST

## EIGHT: DIVINE INTERRUPTIONS

## NINE: AN INVASION BY GOD

## TEN: THE UNINVITED GUEST

## PART 1

# WHERE

# IS

# JESUS?

# CHAPTER 1

# WHERE JESUS IS

In 1948 little Wally was small enough to crawl under the church pews, young enough to be hauled up one-handed by his mother. At the same time, he was old enough to suffer a spiritual crisis. Wally had never seen Jesus with his own eyes. Surely, the Savior should be strolling through the rooms of God's house.

Wally was convinced that all the other Sunday worshipers had seen the Lord face-to-face or they wouldn't be singing hymns without anxiety, nor would they merely murmur their prayers. They didn't have to shout, for *their* Jesus was nearby, wearing a robe and a rope and sandals, eating sandwiches, and drinking soda pop.

Maybe Jesus was hiding from Wally particularly. Maybe he was mad at Wally for some sin. But *what* sin? Wally couldn't remember. But *shouldn't* a kid remember a sin so bad that Jesus would reject him? Wally tried hard to remember so that he could say that he was very, very sorry.

The preacher preached gobbledygook. During his sermons, then, little Wally slipped from the pew-seat to the floor and peered through a forest of anklebones and pant cuffs and shoes and shoelaces. No dice. Not long and his mother grabbed him by the shirt collar, dragged him to the pew, and clapped him to her side with an incontrovertible grip.

She was a very strong woman, his mother, and her will was absolute. Once in Glacier National Park a ranger said, "You meet a bear, give him the right-of-way. Don't look into its eyes. Don't run. Move slowly, slowly away."

When Virginia *did* meet a bear coming out of the woods and ambling toward her tent, she went after it, whacking two pans together and yelling, "Not *my* kids!"

The bear said, "Woof," and turned away.

But Wally, he remained obdurate.

*I wanted to see Jesus!*

One Sunday, then, he clutched his crotch and jiggled. He said to his mother, "I got to go pee."

She said, "If you have to, you have to. But come straight back."

✦ ✦ ✦

The heart of a child is capable of great desolation—and thereby of great cunning. The more I felt abandoned, the sharper became my baby wit, trying to figure out where Jesus was concealing himself. I thought I might catch him off guard in, say, the pastor's office. I looked there but found him not. I looked into the roaring boiler room. In the church kitchen. In the boy's bathroom. And then, with a fearful thrill, I ventured the Holy of Holies, the girl's bathroom. Boys never passed it by without spasms of awe.

The room had the aroma of woman-mystery. Along one wall was a counter before which were small cushioned stools, on which were little spray bottles of perfume and boxes of Kleenex, and behind which was an elaborate, wood-framed mirror, but no Jesus. On the other hand, there were two metal potty stalls. Nervously I swung their doors open, one after the other—then returned to my mother, a gaunt, lost little boy.

The next thought that occurred to me was downright brilliant.

When the pastor turned to face the altar and began to chant, I couldn't believe that the deep bass voice was his. This was a pale, bespectacled man, too short and too mild to produce such a voice. So what? So he was only *pretending* to chant. That voice had to be the glory of the Lord! Now, the altar was a long, wooden affair, shaped something like a coffin. *That's* where Jesus was hiding.

As soon as the service had ended and the people were filing out of church, I crept up the chancel steps and tiptoed to the altar. Then, suddenly, I jumped *(booga-booga!)* behind it. Lo, the altar had no back to it. A dusty floor, an old hymnal, a broken chair, but no Jesus. My Lord was not lying in there, reading the Bible or sipping orange juice.

The heart of a child can grow heavy with sorrow and cold with loneliness. I knew that I was not a pretty boy. "Moon-faced" was what my mother called me. "Wooly-headed." Maybe I was an embarrassment to look at.

My life was over.

✦ ✦ ✦

Sometime later again, during the same worship service, I noticed for the first time what my mother must have been doing all the years of my life.

The ghostly preacher faced the altar and said, "Bread," and then he said, "My body." Everyone was standing. My mother was standing.

The preacher said, "Blood. Drink."

Gruesome.

The preacher turned to us and said, "The peace of the Lord," and everyone sang, "Amen."

Then a man came up the aisle telling the people in each pew that they should go on and walk into the chancel. There was a railing between the people and the pastor, and a long cushion on the people's side where they could kneel. The pastor was moving along that rail.

When it was our pew's turn I noticed a change in my mother. Her head was bowed and her hands were folded, you know, like the angel in our stained-glass window. Like everyone else at the rail, she knelt. But the most astonishing thing was that when the pastor came to her, she put out her tongue and the pastor stuck a little cracker to it, and my mother chewed and swallowed—just like a baby eating Pablum! Then he tipped a big golden cup to her lips. A sippy cup! And Virginia Wangerin drank! This was not the woman who could scare bears. This was not the mother so strong that she could haul a kid right off the floor with one hand only. This was—this was different from anything I'd seen before. I mean *everything* was different.

When she came floating back to our pew, my mother's face was beatific, was the face of an innocent little girl.

And when she sat down beside me, my mother *smelled* different. It was as if she'd come back in a cloud of a mystic, rich aroma. She sat down, bowed her head, and began to move her lips. Praying, I thought. I kneeled on the pew-seat and put my nose close to her face. She looked up at me with that old irritation, but I said, "What's that?"

She said, "What's *what*?"

"That smell," I said. "That smell in your nose?"

"Oh, *that*," she said. "It's what I drank."

"What did you drink?"

"Wine, Wally."

"No," I said, "what's that *inside* of you?"

Virginia sat a while in thought. Then she said, "Blood. It's the blood of Jesus. *Jesus* is inside me."

Oh, my Jesus! My *mother* is your room!

After all the people had finished kneeling and eating and sipping, and when all were in their pews again, we stood up and sang, "Lord, now lettest thou thy servant depart in peace according to thy word—for mine eyes have *seen* thy salvation . . ."

CHAPTER 2

◦◦◦

# A BUNCH-BACKED
# OLD WOMAN

On a raw March afternoon I took my daughter to St. Patrick's Cathedral in Manhattan. I had been lecturing and giving readings in the church where President George Washington is reputed to have worshiped.

In those days I had promised to take my children on a travel-trip, each by each, wherever I'd been invited to lecture: Joseph to St. Louis, Matt to a Bulls' game in Chicago, Talitha to San Francisco and Alcatraz. So now it was Mary's turn. She was ten years old.

The vast, vaulted sanctuary took my breath away. As for Mary, she was simply curious. She said, "Where's Jesus?"

The space echoed with the distant voices of companies of people: tourists wandering about with cameras looped around their necks; students taking notes; devout nuns kneeling and counting their beads and murmuring prayers; priests moving their lips, mumbling Mass in the side chapels, looking to me like black, solitary, lonely, and melancholy figures; and the homeless who had staked claims to tiny territories, lying under worn-out coats, beside grocery bags filled with their few possessions.

Of course they would be here. It was a biting weather outside, and though St. Patrick's was not much warmer, it gave protection against the ripping New York winds.

Actually, I had not brought my daughter here to sightsee. I wanted to teach her things like the cruciform architecture, the Bible stories in the stained-glass windows, the marble columns, the carvings of saints, the symbols and the traditions of the ancient Church.

We moved slowly up the left side of the nave.

"Nave," I said. "That word comes from a Latin word that means 'ship.' Sometimes Christians thought of their churches like big boats floating on the waves of a bad world. The boats kept them safe from the sea-swells of wickedness and danger and war. They were sailing, you see, to the shores of heaven."

Mary nodded. Maybe she understood. Maybe not. She said, "Where's Jesus?"

I pointed to banks of slender, fire-flickering tapers, spilling a watery light on the sand that held them upright. I said, "See those candles, Mary? Each one signifies—I mean, stands for—a prayer that someone is praying, prayers for themselves or for someone else."

The voices in the cathedral merged into one long sigh, as if the stone walls were moaning. The sound reminded me of the enormous waiting room in Union Station in Chicago, where a frightened little boy was watching for his father to come in after getting off the train. Reminded me of the sourceless voices that diminished that boy almost to a kitten.

Now I took Mary by the hand and led her to the statue of a saint standing on a plinth. His eyes were cast to the heavens. His arms were extended, and he wore nothing but a loincloth. Maybe fifty arrows had pierced his body.

"That's a martyr," I said. "People think that martyrs were early Christians that died for their faith. Those people aren't wrong. But that word *martyr* really means 'witness.' That man, the way he died—do you see how his face is not afraid?—he was witnessing before his killers about the love and the power of the Lord. Me too, Mary," I said. "And you too. We don't actually have to *die* to witness about Jesus. It's how we *live*."

Mary listened. The little girl nodded. But I think that she was mostly being nice to her daddy and patient with his highfalutin education.

And on and on. I showed her fourteen separate marble sculptures of Jesus, each one picturing him as he suffered along his way to the cross. And one where he died. And one where his dead body was lying on the lap of his mother, Mary.

"These are called stations," I said. "Catholics walked from carving to carving, praying and thinking about Jesus's story. That one there is called the 'Pietà.' The pity."

Mary said, "Daddy?"

I said, "Just a little while longer. Then we'll go to Burger King. But first you *have* to see the altar."

Directly under the lofty, ribbed, and vast dome of the cathedral, elevated on a marble platform which was partially surrounded by a bronze grill and below which were five round steps up, stood the high altar, grand and impassive.

But something else caught my eye. Some*one* else, actually: a woman sitting on the lowest step. Homeless, obviously; a pendulous bottom lip; her nose swollen like an aging fallen apple. The woman's head was enormous, wearing a man's fedora, yet she was herself short and bunch-backed. A sort of Disney dwarf. Her complexion was brown. Weather-beaten? Perhaps. Unwashed, surely. She wore combat boots and three or four sweaters. Her shoulders were borne down by weariness.

This was nothing I wanted to explain to my daughter. So I led her into the ambulatory, the hemispheric aisle that ran behind the high altar. There were no tourists in this place. Those we moved among were quietly reverential. Nuns in their black habits walking in softly swishing shoes. Several monks wore black robes cinctured at the waist, their hands folded at the stomachs, and their hoods pulled forward, hiding their eyes. A child in white gloves pressed against her mother's skirts.

Mary looked around. The silence itself seemed to have widened her blue eyes. Apparently this place was accomplishing what I had not. It held her whole attention.

At the apex of the semicircular ambulatory was the gate into the Mary Chapel and the adoration of the Virgin. A gentle veneration suffused the room. I entered with my Mary. Attached to the gate frame inside was a coin box for the poor. We sat down, my daughter and I, on small wooden chairs. She was quite content. I was glad to be off my feet. I thought to turn my mind to prayer. Maybe I did, then, pray.

We spent about ten minutes in that place. In the end it was I who chose to leave.

I was a bit surprised to see that the bunch-backed woman had been sitting behind us, and that she had risen too. Her legs must have been sore in spite of her small size. We had to wait behind her while she took mincing steps to the gate. She paused. She fumbled through the pockets of a sweater, then brought out a number of coins and put them in the poor-box. She crossed herself and left the chapel.

A witness, she was, walking the Way of the Cross. Perhaps the shafts of the fifty arrows of old age and poverty piercing her soul.

"Mary," I whispered. "There he is. There is Jesus ahead of us. In that woman."

PART 2

# JESUS

# DRAWING

# NEAR

# CHAPTER 3

# TALITHA: GRANDMA TRULA'S PRAYERS

The Apostle Paul writes to the saints at Colossae that even in his absence he has "never ceased to pray for you." This is a piece of that prayer: "May you be strengthened with all power according to his glorious might, for all endurance and patience and joy."

Ever since Paul had heard the voice of the Lord on the way to Damascus; ever since the scales had fallen from his eyes; ever since he had been baptized, Saint Paul prayed for people far away. Faithfully, he believed that the Holy Spirit would bear the Lord's responses across lands and seas to the friends whom Paul named in his prayers.

And Saint James underscores what prayer can do. In his letter "To the Twelve Tribes in the dispersion," he writes, "The prayer of a righteous man has great power in its effects." A righteous man, James writes—but in this case I must write, "A righteous *woman*."

Trula had never seen her birth grandbaby, not until she met Talitha at that girl's graduation from Spelman College in Atlanta, Georgia.

In those days adoption papers were sealed absolutely. The names of the birth family were not given to the adoptive family, nor the adoptive family's names to the birth family. Trula, then, had not known the name of her birth granddaughter, nor where she lived, nor anything about the child's life.

"Talitha," I said to the elderly woman while we were sitting on a bench at the base of Stone Mountain. "We took that name from Mark's gospel where Jesus raises a little girl from her deathbed, saying, 'Talitha, cumi.' We named our baby girl 'Talitha Michal.'"

And Trula said, "Her first mama named her Cassindra Marie."

Then she told me that she had been praying for her unknown grandbaby through the last twenty years.

The prayer of a righteous woman availeth much. Talitha had grown into a healthy, bold, and self-asserting woman. Unlike her sister Mary, she kept a clean bedroom. She maintained a tight schedule. If anyone woke her when that schedule required her to be sleeping, she would become the falcon that catches ducks in its talons.

✦ ✦ ✦

During her early years I would look at my daughter across the dinner table and blur my eyes, seeking the features of her begetters. These seemed always to hover ghostly over her, their faces indistinct. We knew that her father was African American and that her mother was white, and that she had been born in Frankfort, Indiana. As Talitha grew up among us, the presence of those souls remained an anonymous, unknown blank.

In May 1993, Thanne and I were driving our daughter south from Valparaiso, Indiana, to Spelman College in Atlanta, Georgia, where she was about to register for her freshman year. Boxes blocked the back window. As we approached Frankfort, Talitha said, "I want to stop here."

I looked at her in the rearview mirror. She was not playing. She was dead serious.

"Really?" I said. "Are you sure?"

She said, "Are you challenging me?"

Thanne said, "Yes, Wally, she's sure. And so am I."

Frankfort is a small town, a nonentity about thirty-five miles northwest of Indianapolis. We had never found reason to drive there before.

Thanne said, "We've been talking, Talitha and I."

"What do you mean, talking?"

I turned onto State Highway 28. While I drove the nine miles to Frankfort, Thanne told me their story.

At some point while Talitha was still in high school, Thanne came upon her in the TV room. The girl was watching an Oprah Winfrey show. Her mother stood behind her. Soon Thanne realized that Oprah was reuniting adopted children with their birth parents. Talitha was sitting on the floor, transfixed. She must have felt her mother's presence, for she said, "I want to find my mother." I don't know whether Thanne felt an apprehensive tug in her stomach. She said to Talitha, "Think this over. Wait till you're eighteen and ask again."

Frankfort was altogether white. Certainly the arrival of a black man nineteen years ago must have caused a stir. Someone might remember him.

We drove to the county courthouse, hoping to find books in which records had been written. No dice. Then to the hospital where Talitha was born. Next to the Lutheran church where we supposed Talitha had been baptized. No one could tell us a thing. No one remembered a black man, and—this was the greatest hindrance—at that time we knew no other name for our daughter than the one we'd given her.

The following summer Talitha and Thanne repeated their searches in Frankfort. This time they spoke with ordinary citizens, always giving out their names and our telephone number. Among those whom they approached was a youngish newspaper reporter.

Shortly after Talitha had returned to Spelman, that same reporter called our house in Valparaiso: "I think I have the name of your daughter's birth-mother's father: Williams. He still lives in Frankfort."

The old ghosts were approaching reality, while I myself felt ever more ghostly. I wondered: the closer and closer our daughter came to finding her birth family, would she also be traveling farther and farther away from us? Yet a parent seeks the wholeness of a child, even as the Creator had conceived that wholeness from the beginning. The parent cannot cling too long or else the relationship is sundered anyway and less happily.

So my wife and my daughter scoured the Frankfort telephone

book until they believed they'd found the right "Williams." They discussed how best to approach the man, and how best to ask for his daughter's address.

Talitha in Atlanta said, "You phone him."

Thanne agreed. But the call would not be easy. She would not lie in order to get the information. But if my wife should mis-speak, she might rake up old grievances. Williams might hang up on her, and the tentative link would be broken.

She dialed the number.

A woman answered. She would turn out to be Mr. Williams's second wife, a gentle creature withal.

Thanne drew breath and asked to speak with the man of the house.

"Just a moment."

Not long and Mr. Williams was on the line. "Yes?"

Thanne said, "I think my daughter knew your daughter years ago."

"Yes?"

"But she lost contact. Would you be willing to give me her address?"

There followed a distinct hesitation. Then the man said, "Wait," and put the receiver down.

His wife must have overheard the conversation. She picked up the phone. "If he doesn't," she said, "or if he won't, just leave it up to me."

Williams returned. "Mary lives in Dallas," he said. *Mary!* "Here's the address." He read it off to Thanne.

Thanne said, "And her telephone number?"

That too he gave to her.

As soon as the call had ended, Thanne called Talitha with the information. This time our daughter chose to make the telephone call herself. Thanne continued to stand by the phone.

When it rang, Talitha snatched it up.

Her voice had the tones of disappointment. She said, "That Dallas number's been disconnected."

And there it was. The long search had failed.

Yet it is precisely here that I saw the hand of God. For while Talitha was visiting Evansville, where we'd lived before, she happened to notice a copy of the Frankfort High School Yearbook on a friend's tea table. Now, since that friend had also gone to Bosse, Talitha asked her husband whether *he* had attended that high school.

"I did," he said.

Talitha's next question: "Did you know a Mary Williams?"

"Only by name," he answered. "She was several classes behind me. Wait," he said. "Her class had a reunion last year. I know someone who has the list of names and addresses."

Not only addresses, but also that class's telephone numbers.

Late that night it was Talitha's turn to call my wife with information. The girl fairly screamed through the line, "I have it! Mary Williams's number!"

Thanne said, "That's wonderful!"

Talitha yelled, "I'm going to call her right now!"

Thanne, the voice of reason, said, "It's the middle of the night. Call her in the morning."

By dawn Talitha could wait no longer. She dialed the number. After five or six rings a woman answered in a croaky voice. "What?"

Talitha said, "Is this Mary Williams?"

"Yes. Why?"

"Did you have a baby girl one night in January 1974?"

There followed a breathing pause. Then, "Who's this?"

Talitha cleared her throat. In a formal voice she said, "I have reason to believe that I am the baby you had."

Another pause, a weighty pause lasting a long, long time.

Talitha said, "If you want, I can call you later."

Mary Williams said, "I always knew you'd call. I just didn't think you'd *wake me up*!"

Later, on her own, Talitha drove from Atlanta to North Carolina to meet her birth father, Carter, who lived with his mother.

✦ ✦ ✦

So then, we were sitting on a picnic bench at the base of Stone Mountain, Talitha's grandmama and I, when I told her why we'd given our daughter her name, and Trula told me that the name she'd been born with was Cassindra Marie.

Thanne sat down on my side of the table.

As we talked, the elderly woman began to speak through tears.

"The baby," she said, "called me grandma today. My baby called me grandma. All these many, many years I been praying for her—" praying for her blood grandbaby ever since the child had disappeared into the dark caves of adoption.

When we had met the white Mr. Williams face-to-face for the first time, we found him to be a rough-hewn man. Yet even he was choking back tears when he said to Talitha, "You are a part of us."

Then it was his wife who proved it so by embracing our daughter.

+ + +

After all, I had not been wrong to seek Talitha's forebears in her face. Mother Mary has the same slant of jaw, the same high cheekbones, the same aggressive manner.

And Thanne and I are no less her parents than we had been before.

So is Mary her parent.

And so is God the Father.

Oh, how wonderful are the wounds and the intrusions of the Lord, whose glory bursts upon us especially at the changings of our lives!

# CHAPTER 4

# WALLY: DREADING CHRISTMAS

In the 1950s the milkman delivered milk to the doors of houses—six bottles in a wire basket, each with a bulge at its neck. As it separated from the milk, the cream rose to fill these bulges. Cream was common in those days. So was butter. But butter was too expensive for our family's budget. My mother bought margarine instead. To protect its dairy farmers, Alberta, Canada, had passed a law requiring margarine to be sold only in its original, unappealing, lard-white color. A button of orange powder was included in each brick-sized box. Mix this powder with the margarine. But don't expect the color to become a true butter-yellow. We children could always see and taste the difference.

The milkman brought his wares along Ada Boulevard in a horse-drawn wagon. Especially in winter Mother said, "Tune your ears to hear his coming." In the cold Canadian air we could hear the kindly congregational clinkings even before the wagon turned onto our street. It was our job to rush outside and bring the bottles in before the cream froze and lifted its hat on an ice-cream column.

"Well, children, how do you do?"

"Just fine, Mr. Cream, and how are you?"

So it was on Christmas Eve Day 1955 that we gathered at our front windows to watch for the mare and her wagon, and for the milkman to come bustling up the front walk. Mother wanted to be shed of us and our wild joy so that she could bake cookies in peace.

The mare moved in a slow walk, treading the hardened street-snow on either side of which banks of snow had been thrown up six feet high, snow banks we would be kings of tomorrow. She came nodding, never stopping while her master rushed up sidewalks, made his delivery, and rushed back again. Her back was blanketed. She blew plumes of steam from her nostrils. Her chin had grown a beard of hoarfrost. We burst from the house. The air was a crystal bowl of cold. The day was perfectly right, and we laughed with happiness.

To tell the truth, it was my siblings who laughed. I didn't. Last year, while we were opening our presents, my brother Paul started sobbing, and then cried outright, though I don't know why. This year and this night, then, I feared that something might un-gladden our celebrations. A high-pitched, tightened excitement is a dangerous thing, for it could be stretched like a rubber band to its breaking point. I was silent and solemn, watchful, and infinitely cautious—an adult at eleven. For what if you hoped and hope failed you? The harder your hope, the more vulnerable you.

By supper, Christmas Eve had become midnight black. We'd bathed. We ate tomato soup in our bathrobes. Then my six brothers and sisters raced bubbling to their bedrooms and dressed. I combed my hair with faucet water. We shrugged into our parkas and went outside to the car.

Immediately my hair froze and crackled when I touched it. We sat three and three and three in the three seats of our Volkswagen minivan. Since its engine gave forth little heat, our breath steamed the windows. Dad said, "Breathe through your ears." This was his regular winter's joke. Finally we crowded into the blazing light of the church.

With a wonderful hilarity, people greeted us with, "Merry Christmas!"

Children were shooed into the fellowship hall to put on their costumes. Oh, how they laughed with excitement. Not me. To laugh is to lose one's self-control.

Then, from the youngest to the oldest, the children tromped into the chancel. The little ones waved to their parents by finger-scratching the air. They positively shined, while their parents smiled and craned left and right in order to see better.

I was God. I told Joseph to travel with his pregnant wife from Nazareth to Bethlehem. A quartet of boys sang "Wonderful Counselor." A teenage fellow in the back of the church blew on his trumpet the "Hallelujah Chorus" of Handel's *Messiah*. So elegant was the music, and so clear, reminding me of a running stream of water, that I was almost moved to tears. *Almost.* I contained the tears as in an iron box.

Every kid was given a brown paper bag filled with tangerines and walnuts and hard candy. The adults, humping into their overcoats, called, "Merry Christmas! Merry Christmas!"

Dad delayed our trip home by driving past those Edmonton houses whose lawns were decorated with lights, and the three kings from the east, and stables, and beasts—and effigies of the Holy Family—intensifying the excitement! Our breath frosted the windows. With my gloved knuckles I rubbed a peephole through the muzzy ice. I saw a tableau of Dickensian carolers cut of plywood, top hats, scarves, muffs on their hands, their mouths open, their eyes screwed up to heaven in a transport of song. But they produced, of course, not a note of music. This was worse than silliness. It was dangerous, for I found my soul suddenly suffering pity for these wooden fictions and their plaintive gladness.

At home Dad delayed even longer. He had hung the tree with silver tinsel and had strung its boughs with colored lights in the room of our final celebrations.

We put on pajamas. It was Dad's tradition to line us up facing him in the kitchen. The line started with Dena, the youngest sister, and ended with the eldest brother. Me. Dena clasped her hands and raised her shining, saintly face to Dad. Her hair hung down her back to her waist. Blithe child! Her blue eyes sparkled with trust.

Dad prayed the prayer he always prayed.

> Ah, dearest Jesus, holy child,
> Make thee a bed, soft, undefiled,
> Within my heart, that it may be
> A quiet chamber kept for thee.

Then he led us to the door of the room of celebrations. I chewed my cheek and frowned like thunder. *No! It won't be what it ought to be. It never is.*

Dad grasped the knob and opened the door upon a string of muted, colored lights. I knew that there were in the room seven piles of presents, one for each of the children. Dena went in ahead of the rest. Squeals of joy. And there sat our mother on the floor in front of the tree, her skirt encircling her, her face radiant and verging on laughter.

I hesitated. So did my father. He was gazing at me. And here was the wonder that was to be fixed in my memory forever—that his gaze was filled with a yearning expectation. He had, just as I had, been withholding whatever joy or excitement he might have been feeling.

"Wally?" he said, and I realized that his solemnity had been on account of *me*. That he too had passed this Christmas Eve day in the hope that risks a hurt. And that, among the promises to which my father had committed his hope and his soul, this was the most important one: that his eldest son should soften and be glad.

If I had grown adult in 1955, then how like a child had my father become.

"Come," he said. I obeyed. We entered the room. The colored lights painted his face with reds and greens and blues. And still he gazed at me, waiting for me to receive Christmas so that his own Christmas might begin.

I began to cry silently. And now I was gazing at my father. Defenseless was I, because there was no more need for defenses. Glad and unashamed was I, because what *was* this room so long locked? It was my heart. And why had I been afraid? Because I thought my heart would be found an empty thing, hard and unfeeling.

But in my father I saw the love that had furnished this Christmas room no differently than he had in past years, except that this year he'd furnished it with a yearning desire.

And what else was that love but my Jesus drawing near?

Look, then, at what I found this room and found my heart to be: a quiet chamber kept for thee. A new Nativity of the Lord.

My dad moved toward me, his arms not at all emptied, for he filled them with myself. He embraced me, and I filled my arms with him.

And so we, the both of us, were filled with joy.

# PART 3

# THE FIERCE

# ANGER

# AMONG

# OURSELVES

## CHAPTER 5

‧ ᴏᴏᴏ ‧

# ARTHUR BIAS:

# "WAN-TER TOSS A LINE?"

R ev?" Arthur Bias, eighty years old if he was a day and rolling into my church study.

"Rev? Wan-ter toss a line this mawnin'?"

Grace Lutheran Church was an inner-city church. My tasks were both *to* my parishioners and on *behalf* of them. This latter task caused me no end of anxiety. Often it placed me at odds with the politicians and the officials of our city. I had no choice but to confront them, both privately and publicly. Two very tall white officers would drive our streets looking for minor infractions. If they thought that some black teenager had sassed them, they got out of their car, their hands on the butts of their guns, and might arrest him on the spot. More than once Officer Tall and Officer Taller came to my house at night, banging on my front door, demanding the whereabouts of this thief or that prostitute.

Rich people tended to avoid Lincoln Avenue because it cut straight through what they called the "ghetto."

Since I was white, and since they believed that I had the ears of white people generally, some of my parishioners looked to me to be their voice against racism. I tried. Even in white churches I named the subtlest gestures, the unconscious attitudes, the tones of voice with which a white person demeaned an African American person.

"Hey!" responded certain white Christians. "I'm not racist. Some of my best friends are black."

Several times a splenetic man or woman telephoned me at home, not at my office, to promise me and my children deadly harm.

It was smack in the middle of these trials and tribulations that Mr. Arthur Bias intruded on my life.

✦ ✦ ✦

I miss you, Arthur, my old, enormous, deep-voiced, droop-jowled, slow-striding, big-bellied black man, and my friend.

You walked a beat in your day, joining the force in the 1950s, strolling the neighborhood through '60s and into '70s. Retired you might have been when we went fishing, but you never retired your stories. They were my salt while we fished together, your eyelids at half-staff, gazing across the river with remembering, the Ohio River to Kentucky. To "Kain-tuck," as you called it, telling your tales with neither guile nor anger, but laughing deep in your chest.

You bottom-fished, declaring that it took the least energy. You let the line hang down from its bobber, a grub or an angleworm on the hook. You caught catfish with pieces of bacon, bullheads with cheese, and carp with anything.

"Wan-ter toss a line, Reverent?"

We were Huck Finn and Black Jim. We used bamboo poles and shaded our faces with the brims of our straw hats. You sat in a banded lawn chair, bulging its bottom to an inch from the ground. You lit your pipe, and slit your eyes, and sometimes stayed silent for long periods at a time. I believed it was the droning flies that had softened your brains to drowsiness. Yours was an uncomplicated world, and God was the giver of lazy afternoons.

When you nodded off you made buzzing sounds in your nose which was as big as a summer squash. Then you'd wake to the tug of a fish, pull it in, hang it on a gill-line, and start another story.

"Never did pull my service revolver more 'n a few times. Never had to. Made my wishes known in t'other ways. Gen'rally knew the whippersnapper's grandmama. In fact, I knew *every* name on my beat, and all the teenagers from their mother's knee. Tol' him I's gonna tell *her*. That did right well."

Yours was a moral authority, as well as the authority of your massive size. You established intimacy first. Then it was the flash of your badge. And then, before a six-inch knife, your authority came from the draw of your gun. A service revolver could vomit wrath and death. But you never, ever planned to pull the trigger.

"Tell you wot," Arthur said. "Them slush-walkin' boys and them gum-snappin' girls did heed me, yes. Didn't much care if a boy like me or no. Ahmmm," Arthur toned in his nose. "If what-choo call a 'juvenile delinquent' didn't come to like me, well, he didn't disrespeck me."

Arthur Bias had made the neighborhood a civil community. He turned a lawman's job into a job of tact and benevolence. The rich folks who avoided Lincoln Avenue did so as blind fools.

Suddenly my red-and-white bobber was dragged under the water. I felt the fish-tug in my hand and a twitch of delight in my gut. I yanked the pole, but too quickly. It cracked in half.

"Still schoolish," Arthur laughed. "Got to learn, Rev."

When he laughed, his shoulders heaved into a seismic quake. And then I did truly believe that the earth itself was quaking and laughing along with this old man.

✦ ✦ ✦

There came the night when Officers Tall and Taller pounded on my front door.

"Where's your boy?" they barked. "Where's Matt?"

We had adopted Matthew when he was an infant. An African American. Now in high school, he kept failing to make it home by his curfew.

"Take it easy," said Taller. "He ain't in trouble. It's that gang he runs with."

Gang? There were no gangs in our city until much, much later.

"Got a call," said Taller.

"Right," said Officer Tall. "We got a witness says he saw a bunch of them underaged bangers drinking behind Doc's Liquor Store. Says they stole his vee-hickle."

"Who says?"

"Privileged information."

"Then who jacked your witness's car?"

"Wears a red tank-top."

As it turned out, the cops arrested three youths on the bare chance that one of them was their criminal.

Matt came home, wide-eyed and scared.

✦ ✦ ✦

I miss you, Arthur.

When you lay dying in Deaconess Hospital, you did not struggle against death. Peaceful walking, peaceful fishing, and peacefully awaiting your end.

Actually, what was most on your mind then was butter beans. You said you liked them best when they'd been cooked in bacon grease with sausages boiled to the point of popping.

In the weeks before you entered the hospital, you wrote notes for your wife. One on the lawn mower, telling Musetta how to oil the machine, to gas it, and to clean it after the grass had been cut. A note on the boiler-furnace. One on the thermo-stat. One on the steering wheel of the car.

Finally, you lost interest in butter beans. In any sort of food, even in a drink of water. Nor was it fishing on a warm summer's day that closed your eyes in silence. It was pleurisy.

Musetta telephoned me. "Ain't long now, Pastor. Arthur's gone to hiccupping, an' Ah'm hearin' the death rattle."

So I came and served you the Lord's last supper.

Musetta said, "He cain't drink nor chew."

But I had a way to commune you. I dipped my finger in the wine and took away a single drop. This I touched to a broken piece of wafer, then touched *that* to your tongue. It was enough. I sat by your bed and read First Corinthians, the fifteenth chapter.

Musetta and I prayed the Lord's Prayer. Through all your years, Arthur, life was its own sufficiency. What you had, you cherished. What you didn't have, you did not desire. Therefore, this evening beside the River of Life was a promise of Eden. And the dawn in heaven was the New Jerusalem.

And still I miss my fisher-friend's conviction that all people are worthy of latitude and honor and downright affection.

# CHAPTER 6

# BLUE-JACK: THE HAMMER OF GOD

The man wore the uniform of a marine. His chest was broad. His jaw jutted out like a rocky shelf, his manner aggressive, and his skin the color of a grand piano.

"You white," he said.

"I am," I said.

He sat in a Buick not looking at me, but staring through the windshield. "You got no bid-ness here-abouts," he said. "Why you walkin' ma streets?"

"I live over on Chandler," I said. "My business is preaching."

"Mm-hmm. Wanna tell another lie on me?"

"It isn't a lie." I gestured to Grace Lutheran. "That's my church."

The man unfolded himself and stepped from his car, leaving the driver's-side door open. "Been a slew of robberies up Gum Street, Brother," he said. "Eliot too. Know anything about that?"

"Well, no. But I'm sorry to hear it."

"Look-it at that there." He pointed at a red-brick, sway-beamed shotgun house three doors down from Grace. "Ma girlfriend rents that there. Done got her TV stole. Not two weeks an' some fool stole her stereo. An' me? Right then I swears I'm gonna patrol the neighborhood."

The marine moved into my personal space. Broad-chested, jut-jawed, he towered over me. The roof of my mouth felt like hard clay. I tried to swallow dry spit. "Well," I said, "good luck at that."

"I see you," he growled, "an' ma luck's done changed. Come here." He walked to the Buick. I stood stock-still. "Come *here!*" and I did. "Look-it down at ma floorboard."

My armpits started to sweat.

"What-choo see?"

Under the right dash lay a very big gun.

".44 Remington Magnum," said the marine. "Calls her ma Menace. *Now* go on an' tell me what bid-ness a white man gots here-abouts—an' I don't want no lies."

I thrust my hand into my pants pocket and pulled out a ring of keys. "Here's proof," I said. "I can unlock the church door."

I turned to do so, but the man said, "Ain't no thing for robbers to make new keys at the hardware store."

The big man bent down and took up the Magnum.

I stifled a groan.

He aimed his gun to the sky and let loose a powerful *BOOM*.

Just then Betty Ferguson, the daughter of Gloria Ferguson, came driving up Gum in a red convertible. She braked beside us. "Blue-Jack!" she scolded the marine. "You still trifling with your pistol, boy?" To me she said, "Pastor, can you spare an hour? Talk with me this afternoon? I got something to get off my chest."

"I," I said, shaking. "Well," I said. "Yes, Betty. I have an hour at three."

"Good," said Betty. "I'll be back then, Reverend," and she drove away.

"Oh, man, oh man," said the marine. "You come a little whisker away." Then he said, "Here, wanna try my Menace?"

"No. No. Thank you."

The big man grinned. That grin slurred his face like a schoolboy's. "So," he said and dived into the back seat. He brought out a black case. He opened it and took out a flute. "Loan me ten bucks, Rev," he said, "an' I'll leave this here at the church till I c'n pay you back."

# PART 4

# GOODS GET GOODNESS, BADS GET BADNESS

CHAPTER 7

〰

# HENRY: HIS GOD FROM
# THE BEGINNING

By the shore of Crawling Stone Lake in northern Wisconsin, there lived a man who must have been seventy-five years old the last time I visited him—visited him after his wife had died. His was a white-frame house, well-kept because he was by nature fastidious—a neat man, but very, very angry.

The lake lapped the pilings of a short dock. The waves rocked the aluminum boat, which he powered with an Evenrude motor. He fished. He scaled his catches and fried or broiled them—not because he needed the food, but because this was the way he spent his retirement. I will call him "Henry."

It was more than a decade ago when Henry and his wife had moved north from Milwaukee. Happy were their days then, she a gardener of flowers and a reader of books; he both stout and vigorous and handy with tools. Though his fingers were blunt, they were quick at tying his own flies. Henry could sweep his rod in long, lacy casts upon the streams nearby: salmon and trout. Or he'd troll the lake in his boat: walleyes, pike, bass, and the burnished sunfish.

We had become friends while they still lived in Milwaukee. No surprise, then, that the two of them invited me to visit them in their new house on Crawling Stone Lake. Henry's wife was still alive. Henry himself asked whether I wanted to go fishing with him. I think he enjoyed the fact that I was a rube at the sport. In those days Henry was expansive, even devout. He and his wife attended a small Lutheran church in Woodruff. She had been the churchgoer. Likely it was for love of his wife more than his love for God that persuaded the stubborn, self-saving husband to worship with her.

I remember a dawn when the lake was absolutely quiet, absolutely still, and covered with mist. We motored into the mist. The sun's rays struck it vermillion. The mist dissolved. The sky became a high blue bowl, and we fished. Henry stood in the boat. He looped a beautiful cast. The lure made a distant *plunk*. Not three minutes later and he gave his rod a small tug.

"First," he instructed me, "set the hook. Give the fish her head. Play out the line." Henry did that. "Slowly, slowly," he said, "reel the line in till it goes taut. Pull the fish around and slowly toward the boat." He did that too and said, "Walt—get the net."

Back at the house Henry showed his wife a string of fish. She smiled and said, "Thank the Lord for little things." He smiled in return and winked at me, "She always does. Lil always says that." I never forgot her words. They seemed to represent her husband's sentiment as well.

During their second year in paradise Lillian contracted pancreatic cancer. Henry nursed her through the months of the wasting disease until she died and left him in the house alone.

It was eight years thereafter that I visited Henry for the last time. By then the widower had become a grim, forbidding, frowning, and most angry man.

Why this anger? An enforced loneliness? Perhaps, but seven years was an awfully long time to maintain grief. Estrangement? Perhaps Henry had loved Milwaukee's environment more than he'd known before his move. From his birth it had shaped him—its clattering, factory noises, the noises of the brakes of its busses and trucks, its rivers of people, the smell of diesel fuel, streets of grit, snow defiled by salt and gravel. Perhaps the northern forests were simply too pristine. Could it have been old age? His own death close at hand? Well, no. The man's heart was healthy, and his strength undiminished. Not poverty nor the gloom at night.

But, as I came to learn in the next several days, his rage was at the Indians.

✦ ✦ ✦

Henry had never met an Indian face-to-face, had never seen fit to meet one in that big city on the shores of Lake Michigan. He was utterly ignorant of their rights, their behaviors, their race, and their culture. Yet Henry was damn sure he knew and could name their many transgressions.

Start with this, that he did not own the land beneath his white-frame house, nor the patch his Lillian had gardened, not one foot of Crawling Stone Lake, nor even the fish he took from the lake. The land and the water and his dock and its pilings belonged to the Lac du Flambeau Indian Reservation. If they wished, the Chippewa could claim it all—and then what? Would they remove him? Drive him back to Milwaukee? Henry had planned to bury his wife beside the house where they had lived so happily. He planned to visit Lillian's headstone every evening to pay his respects. With what anger, then, did he learn that the Indians refused to allow anyone but themselves to be buried in the earth of their reservation. And anger became downright hatred when Henry had no other choice but to bury his wife among her relatives in the cemetery of a Lutheran church in Milwaukee.

Before his retirement, my friend had worked for the Miller Brewing Company. Consequently he had always preferred beer to stronger spirits. On Sunday morning I attended church alone. At noon he offered me a drink of Canadian whiskey. That night he took me to the end of his dock.

"Damn them!" he said. "They're at it again."

Across the lake I saw beams of light shifting this way and that. Flashlights, so I supposed—narrow spotlights reflecting off the surface of the calm lake. I heard the bumping of boats. The air carried back men's voices speaking contentedly in a language I couldn't understand. Periodically I heard a thrashing of water.

Henry was seething. "Spear-fishing," he hissed. "This is April. The white man's season don't start till May when walleye and northern pike are done spawning!" And as if that weren't enough, my exasperated friend cried, "At night, by God! With *lights*! Illegal to me, but to the Indians . . ."

We returned to the house. This time I accepted his offer of a shot of Canadian whiskey. Henry drank from a tall water glass with a single cube of ice. He sat in a well-worn easy chair, crouching like a crow on the branch of a dead maple tree.

Beer used to make Henry garrulous. Whiskey made him silent—and morose.

I tried several topics, none of which he responded to. Finally, I shut up.

Then Henry growled, "But I'm ready for them." He wasn't looking at me. His eyes were interior, his eyelids and his cheeks gone red.

I said, "Ready for what?"

He said, "When them Indians come busting through the door, by God, I'm ready for them!" He stood up. "Come and look," he said. "I'll show you what I call my Readiness."

He went into the bedroom.

He reached under his pillow and pulled out an old SIG Sauer pistol. He released the clip and said, "My P228. Loaded. I'm ready for them."

Henry's hostility was almost religious. It was also irrational. All of his sorrows he had named by that one false name only: "Indian."

✦ ✦ ✦

Whether my old friend Henry believed in him or not, Lillian's God was his God too. *Had* been his God from the beginning. And was, by the divine love of the wood-crossed Christ, his God still. If Henry could not pray with the Psalmist, I could. I did. I do.

# CHAPTER 8

# TALITHA: DO ME A FAVOR AND DIE

A "shotgun house" is usually constructed with three rooms back to back to back. Whether it had three rooms or more, there was always a hallway running in a dead-straight row from the front door to the back. It might well be that the house is named for this hallway, for I've heard it said that one could shoot a shotgun through and through the house without nicking the wood.

In those days my family and I lived seven short blocks from Grace Lutheran Church. It would take me no more than fifteen minutes to walk the distance, which I did most Sundays by myself, arriving at church around five-thirty a.m. in order to pace the sanctuary, searching for the shape and the words of the sermon I would preach at ten o'clock.

But there came the morning when a man from Zimbabwe,

Africa, a Reverend Farai Gambiza, was scheduled to take my place in the pulpit. Because I was relieved of that pastoral duty, I didn't leave home until nine. Talitha chose to walk along with me. Well, as a matter of fact she walked in the street just off the curb. It has often amused me that a child wants to prove her independence by breaking some little rule—unaware that *many* children and *many* teenagers consider themselves each the only individual bold enough to break that rule. Hence my daughter, repeating the pattern, knew not that she was following a crowd—not at all an individual.

The weather was fair. The cars were few. And Talitha was a bonny little girl. Her complexion was caramel-colored, a mix of the skins of her black birth father and her white birth mother. When Thanne and I had adopted her, she was eight months old, her head shaped like a lightbulb, on the top of it a scribble of black hair. Her eyebrows were dark, her brow wide, her lashes long and luxurious. The baby's lips made a pink bow. Nowadays my daughter's hair was considered "good" because it was not nappy but soft and straight. Her movements were delicate and her skin unblemished. As she was walking in the street, she did not hold my hand.

Ahead of us was a series of shotgun houses.

✦ ✦ ✦

Suddenly I heard from one of those houses a growl so deep I thought it was a man's. Talitha must have heard it too. She slowed her steps to a cautious walk. But the voice had not been a man's. When we were about three yards from the house, its front screen door was banged open. A boy flew out, landing on his bum. Next a woman stood on the porch, barefooted and wearing pajamas. She pointed her finger at the boy-child and screamed, "Do me a favor! Do me a favor—and die!"

Then she turned and slammed back into the house. The boy sat blinking on the sidewalk. I estimated that he was a year older than my daughter.

My daughter. She had watched the whole incident standing stock-still. Then, of her own accord, Talitha began to move forward. I don't think the boy saw her approaching, for when she had reached him, she said, "It's okay." She touched his shoulder. "You can come with us." The kid was startled. He jumped up. But as soon as he recognized that this was just a little girl, he pointed his finger at her and yelled, "Do me a favor! Do me a favor and die!" He took to his heels and ran down an alley.

Me—I wanted to catch the kid and shake him till his teeth chattered.

But Talitha said, "He's sad."

"Sad or not," I barked, "I'm going to have words with his mother!"

"No, Daddy," said my daughter. "She's sad too. I think it's because she's got no love."

✦ ✦ ✦

"You have heard that it was said, 'You shall love your neighbor and hate your enemy.' But I say to you, 'Love your enemies and pray for those who persecute you.'"

# CHAPTER 9

# KARL: THE SCAR IN MY ANCIENT MARINER'S HEART

generally do my grocery shopping on Friday nights after attending a meeting that lets out about nine thirty. The store is mostly empty then, and I have the aisles to myself, but not *altogether* to myself.

Recently I noticed an elderly man in the produce department, scratching his bewhiskered chin and gazing into a bin of Red Delicious apples. He wore a baseball cap pulled so low that his ears stuck out. Stitched above its bill was the name "Karl," and on the back of his jacket was a picture of a snorting bull. An ancient pair of pants, and on his feet a pair of new, purely white running shoes with swooshes on their sides. Karl's expression was gloomy. I had steered my cart to a pyramid of oranges.

Suddenly the old man grabbed the frame of my cart.

"Fella?" he said. "Fella, you got a minute?"

"Not really," I said.

But he held on as if I'd said nothing at all.

"Them red apples allus do me this away," he said. Still gazing into the bin, Karl sucked his cheeks into hollows, then puffed them out. "Them apples make me so mad, I just wanna *pop*."

He released my cart. He picked up one of the apples and, like the step-mother in *Snow White*, held it up between us. "Just *pop*," he said, and I saw that he lacked two upper teeth. A single lower tooth fit in the gap. I figured he was angry because he favored apples but couldn't get a good bite.

Not so.

"Lookee here. Was Father Ender tuck us on a sightsee trip. Ay-talia. Rome, and such. The priest says, 'No good tryin' to get a look o' the Pope.' Saw the Vat-kin, though."

"The Vatican," said I.

"Yeah. You got that right, son. The Vat-kin. Was all these saints on top o' that there big church. Paint-pictures everywhere inside. The walls, even the ceiling. Little color-stones in the floor. Pretty."

"Forgive me," I said. "It's late. I have to go."

*He holds me with his glittering eye.*

"Went to see some crumbly parts o' the city. And wha'd I see on the way? Folks selling vegetables. Was tent-shops set up along the streets. A man could buy tiny little pizza things, an' trinkets, an' necklaces with crosses o' Jesus on them. An' *fruits*. I'm here to tell you, fella! Apples shiny red and big as cantaloupes!"

Karl replaced the Red Delicious into the bin.

"Me, I laid out a fist-full of Ay-talian money. Bought, swear to God, best an' biggest apple of the lot. Wasn't three days later an' here we was back on the bus, drivin' to the plane bound for New York City, an' me with my apple in a brown paper sack."

My ancient mariner's ears grew pink. His voice grew angry again.

"Gonna take it home, you know? Show the folk at St. Mary's. My mouth already waterin'."

"This guy!" Karl growled. "Was this guy sittin' next to me. Says, 'What-choo got in that bag? Lunch?'"

"Well, an' me all tickled to let him see my big red apple, so I pulled it out."

Karl's old face was sugared with whiskers. He pulled off his baseball cap and with his sleeve wiped the sweat from his brow, puffing and blowing, puffing and blowing.

"Wasn't but a secont an' that there guy! Says to me, 'Lunch.' He . . . he takes my apple. He's got a penknife. Cuts a slice, and don't he just go an' *eat* it!

"Fella," the old man said. "Fella, ain't never been so boilin' mad! No, not never before. I says to him, 'Hey!' but he goes on, slice after slice right down to the core."

We seemed to be the only two customers in the grocery store.

Karl slammed the baseball cap back on his head. "Know what that guy, he says to me? Says, 'What's a apple for, 'cept to eat it?'"

✦ ✦ ✦

The scar in my ancient mariner's heart was lasting and deep, though the cut had been quick and unconsidered. I have no doubt that his assailant forgot the gesture even before the bus reached the airport. It had been nothing to him. Is it so with us?

> Only where love and need are one,
> And the work is play for mortal stakes,
> Is the deed ever really done
> For Heaven and the future's sakes.

ROBERT FROST, "TWO
TRAMPS IN MUD TIME"

# CHAPTER 10

*ᴐᴐᴐ*

# MATTHEW: GOODS GET GOODNESS, BADS GET BADNESS

When Millie, our next-door neighbor, told my wife that she didn't want Matthew to play with her daughter any more, I didn't argue.

Well, little "Peach," as her parents called her, was a delicate, breakable child of small bones and wispy blonde hair and blue veins in her cream-white skin, while Matthew was frolicsome—up with the sun, loud and laughing and out the door, racing across our two-acre field like a sheepdog. He loved the grass and speed and freedom.

Behind the house we'd planted a strawberry bed as long and as narrow as a green rug. When the strawberries were ripe, red, and fat, Matthew, on one of his early morning runs, would throw himself belly-down on the near end of the bed and slide all the way to the other, then smear his face with the fruit. He flew on wings of delight. His actions were unrestrained, and his glee was splendid. In those days he called himself "the six millions dollar man." Sometimes when I came through the front door into the house, Matthew would leap from the back of the sofa and land like a cat on my shoulders.

But I wished that my child would learn self-discipline. That's why I didn't argue with Millie when she separated her daughter and my son.

"That boy is out of control!" she said.

But it made Matthew very sad.

He asked me whether he could carry a bowl of strawberries over to Peach.

"No," I said. "I don't think she can be your friend anymore."

"But," he said, "then she don't have a friend."

I took the opportunity to teach him. We were standing below the land on which our house had been built, standing in a field of yellow flowers. Actually, the flowers were weeds because the soil was alkaline. But the yellow was profuse. The "flowers" seemed to me to be terribly beautiful, for that my brown son stood in their midst.

I said, "Matthew, you have to think of other people first. If you don't, they go away. Walk before you run. Think before you act. Listen before you talk. Whisper before you shout."

Well, I doubt that he was listening then. He kept gazing at the neighbor's house.

"My fault," he said.

I said, "Maybe Peach's mother will change her mind in the future."

✦ ✦ ✦

We teach our children the Law of Fairness. It's important that we do. A self-centered child is likely to become a marauding adult. We train our children to be selfless, or their selfishness will get them in trouble.

"Play by the rules," we say, "so that you have friends who will like you and trust you. Good gets goodness," we say, "and bad gets badness back."

And we say, "If you break the law the world will punish you. But if you obey the law, all will be well."

And all would be well—if the world itself obeyed the Law of Fairness.

Our officers of the law do not play fair with African American teenage boys. Matthew is African American. What will he do when he experiences unfairness?

Nor are teachers always fair with their students—though they may be totally unaware of their mild prejudices. When they ask a question of a white girl, they are willing to wait a long time for an answer. This is because they expect that the right answer will come. When the question is asked of a white boy or a black girl, they don't wait quite as long. But if they have questioned a black boy, they scarcely wait at all, because they don't believe that the right answer will be forthcoming. And what is the consequence? Black boys have no reason to learn, for they can get by *without* learning. So school becomes a dismal waste of time, and specific exams increase their carelessness because they always fail.

✦ ✦ ✦

It couldn't have been more than a month when Thanne called me at church.

"Come home," she said. "I know why Millie rejected our son."

"Right. Because he's hyperactive."

"No." There was an urgency in Thanne's voice. "Just come home."

I didn't think—as Matthew once said to me—"two thoughts." Twenty minutes and I was home. Thanne met me in the kitchen. She told me her story, ending by stating the true reason for our neighbor's intransigence: "It's because Matthew is black."

I set my jaw and walked from our yard to Millie's house and knocked on her door. She opened it and smiled, and I was taken aback by her genuine cordiality.

"Reverend Wangerin," she said. "Come in. I'll put on a pot of coffee."

I followed her inside. She motioned me to a chair and left me alone for a moment, then returned, sat, and folded her hands. "So. What brings you here?"

"To tell the truth," I said, "I want to talk about my son."

"Oh," said Millie in a sort of conspiratorial sadness, "it's too bad, isn't it?"

"Yes," I said.

"Too bad for little negro boys. Their lives must be pretty hard, you know, that makes them turn to alcohol and stealing and all. I feel sorry for them, I do."

"But you—don't you know that it's people like *you* who make their lives hard? My son is too young to suffer prejudice! Why did you cut him off?"

"Don't you know, Reverend Wangerin?" She clucked her tongue and shook her head in pity. "Because black and white don't marry."

# PART 5

## IT'S THE

## LITTLE

## THINGS

# CHAPTER 11

# DIANE: WHAT IF I CAN'T FORGIVE?

It's the little things.

Time was, I used to drive aggressively. It frightened my wife. As if there were a brake on her side of the car, Thanne would stomp hard when I would blow through a yellow traffic light. If I was waiting at a red light with but one car ahead of me, and if its driver hesitated a few seconds after the light had changed to green, oh, I laid on the horn. "Drive, sucker! Wake up and go!"

Let some idiot cut me off on a double-lane highway, and I fulminated. Completely unforgiving, I would punish the idiot by following him bumper to bumper. Thanne would yelp, "What if he stops? You'll get us killed! We have half an hour. What's your hurry?" I wouldn't answer her but would set my jaw. Walt, King of the Road! Sovereign of the Streets! Monarch of the Highways! I never gave a thought to whether the driver was an old woman.

As far as I was concerned, in those days young men were always my adversaries. At the end of the trip Thanne would be wrung out, or else angry at me. I met anger with grim silence.

It was the little sins that caused me to make my own *big* sins.

✦ ✦ ✦

"When I was twelve years old," said the woman sitting across the table from me, "my father began to lie with me."

*Lie with me.* She'd used the biblical phrase as if she were wearing a black, high-necked, down-to-her-ankles Victorian dress. Instead her clothes were summer-light, shorts and a tie-dyed shirt.

"We lived in an old, very large house," she said. "Three bedrooms so spacious that our voices echoed. I felt like such a little girl then. I had three brothers. Two were four and five years older than me, and the third was four years younger."

I will name the woman "Diane." I had never met her before.

I'd been lecturing in Holden Village, an old mining town tucked high in the Cascade Mountains in the state of Washington. I'd taken as my topic "The Silent Women of the Old Testament." One: Leah, Jacob's first wife who suffered the indignities of her husband's love for her sister. Two: Jephthah's daughter who suffered the consequences of her father's ill-conceived oath to sacrifice unto the Lord God whatever living creature met him when he came home victorious, whether a sheep or a goat or a calf. But it was his daughter who welcomed him home. Though he grieved it, Jephthah kept his vow. He sacrificed the girl. Three: Tamar, the daughter of King David, who was raped by David's eldest son.

It was during the Tamar part of the lecture that Diane raised her hand like a schoolgirl.

"Tamar was beautiful," she said. "I get that. But what do you mean by saying she wore a robe with long sleeves? Why *sleeves*?"

"Remember Joseph's coat of many colors? *It* had long sleeves. A mark of his high state in his father Jacob's eyes. Well, the virgin daughters of King David revealed *their* high state by wearing sleeves. Tamar was a virgin and the inhabitant of the king's palace. You can understand how the rape desolated her."

"Desolated?" said my interlocutor.

"Yes. *Desolated* means 'shamed. Cast out. Abandoned.'"

Diane leaned forward. "It's more than shame," she said. "It's guilt. The girl who's been raped thinks it's *her* fault. And worse than being abandoned by other people, she abandons even her own self."

Diane had an easy, disheveled manner. Her tie-dyed shirt was clean but rumpled. She was an unself-conscious woman, smiling and approachable. But after the lecture, when I found her sitting at a dining room table, she wasn't smiling. Her eyes were sad and inward.

She said, "Our house was painted pure white. Trimmed with gingerbread. You might say it was elegant—on the outside, I mean. Not on the inside."

I liked Diane. Her tan was tawny. Her hazel eyes could twinkle with laughter. Just now they were thoughty and dark. Dark with intelligence, but dark. Maybe thirty years old? She had never married.

It surprised me that she was taking me into her confidence. I'd never seen her before, yet she seemed to take me as a counselor. Well, a pastor, I suppose, to whom she could reveal things most private.

She said, "The worst desolation is to believe that God too has abandoned the child who has been raped."

I said, "Why don't I get us some coffee." Holden's dining hall always kept two large urns full and hot. I thought that in the interval Diane might decide to quit her story right then and there. Too terrible to go on. I feared that I was imposing.

But when I returned with two cups of coffee, she said, "How do I know these things? My father lay with me when I was twelve, night after night until I turned sixteen."

"Oh, Diane, then it was you who knew abandonment. Even from God."

"I thought so."

"Are you sure you want to tell me these things?"

She gazed into the full cup. After a moment, without looking up, she said, "Sixteen years old. It was not long after my father was finished that my brothers began to creep into my bedroom at night."

I wanted to take her hand. I said, "Remember what Jesus said to his disciples. 'I am with you always, even to the end of the world.' Listen, Diane. I have no doubt that there were women disciples on that mountain with the twelve apostles. Mary Magdalene. Joanna. Susanna."

Diane said, "It's okay, you know."

"Rape is *never* okay."

"No. I mean, it's okay to tell you these things."

"Your coffee's getting cold."

"The first time my father lay down beside me on my bed, I smelled his sweat. He was moaning. I thought that he was sick. I thought he was crying. But then he got on top of me. He hurt me, then got up and went out of the room. Not a single word. Through all those four years he never said a word to me. Did his business and left me alone. For years after that a man's sweat-smell—even if we were just passing each other on the street—made me want to cry."

It was then that I took hold of Diane's hand, and she did not deny me.

"Who was there I could talk to?" she said. "My mother washed my mouth out with soap. The pastor and everyone else in town respected my father."

Diane's eyes lost focus. She spoke in a voice of baby-wonder.

"When he came into me I would crawl out of my body and go someplace else. The school library where I liked to read books. *Little House on the Prairie.*"

Her eyes returned to me. "Walt, listen to this. I had long glossy hair in those days. My mother used to hum little hymns when she brushed it. My father used to stroke it. But when my brothers . . ." Diane paused. She took a sip of the coffee, cold by now, then set the cup down and said, "I chopped off clumps of my hair. Scissored patches purely bald.

"All those years I was praying to Jesus, 'Love me, love me, love me.'"

Our hands were still linked across the table. I said, "Did Jesus answer your prayer?"

"Well," she said, then said nothing more.

At three o'clock in the afternoon it began to rain outside. Once upon a time Holden had been a mining town. The copper tailings were still heaped giant-high at the edge of the village.

This rain was too light to raise the stream that gave the village its water, but it had, once or twice in the past, overflowed.

Diane said, "No one ever mentioned the secret in our house. I was estranged in the midst of my own family."

She released my hand. She tipped her head, listening to the rain pattering against the window glass.

She said, "The summer before my little brother entered his freshman year in college—that was the year I was going to graduate—Teddy took me for a country ride in his jalopy. Did I tell you we lived in Gig Harbor? Well, when we reached Penrose Park, Teddy pulled to the side of the road and turned off the ignition. He just sat there with his hands on the steering wheel, staring out the windshield.

"After a little while he said to me, 'I remember the times when Dad visited you in your bedroom at night.'

"My heart stopped. He knew! My baby brother had known all along!

"He said, 'Oh, Diane, I'm sorry. I am so sorry that I didn't do anything. That I didn't tell anyone.'

"So then I was caught between two feelings. On the one hand I thought, *What could he have done? He was ten years old.* On the other hand I was so angry I wanted to slap him.

"He said, 'I hated Dad then. I hate him now.'

"Walt!" said Diane, "it was then that I realized that it had *not* been my fault.

"But I refused to speak another word to him, no, not even to my brother Teddy, until he left for college. But I confronted everyone else in the household, father, mother, my two older brothers. I gave voice to that little girl they had wounded. Then

I left them behind to stew in the soup of their sins. I never went home again. Thanksgiving, Christmas, Easter—they could all just go to smash.

"After I graduated, I took a job teaching elementary kids in Seattle. But something kept nagging at me, unsettling me, though I didn't know what it was."

By now we'd been sitting in the dining room for three hours. The village cooks had begun to work in the kitchen. The food sent out a scent that made my stomach growl.

Generally Holden served meatless meals, except on the one day of the week when the cooks grilled bratwurst and frankfurters on the patio outside. This was not that day. Lentils tonight. Diane was still speaking. I blamed myself for letting my mind wander.

She was saying, "I attended church in Seattle. Old habits, I suppose. After the services the pastor did what pastors do. He stood in the church doorway shaking hands. One Sunday he hurried down the aisle and out of the church ahead of his parishioners, and grabbed my hand to shake it, but held it a little too long. My tendency was to jerk my hand away. But his was a tight grip. He asked me what was wrong.

"'Nothing,' I said.

"'Not nothing,' he said to me. 'I've seen how you sit crumpled in the last pew, and I've seen how you slip out during the final hymn.'

"I don't know. Was it the gentleness of his voice? Or his insight into my condition? Something melted inside of me, and my eyes filled with tears.

"He said, 'Why don't I come and visit you tomorrow?'

"Well, that was a little too close to the bone. I said, 'No. I'll come to your office.'

"And I did that, sure to bring a handkerchief.

"The pastor said, 'Your name is Diane. Am I right?'

"I nodded.

"His shelves were jammed with books. He motioned me to a chair. Do you know what he said then? He said, 'Diane, you remind me of Ophelia.' *Ophelia?* That was a strange way to start a conversation. But then the pastor began to explain himself. 'There's a scene in Shakespeare's tragedy,' he said, 'when Hamlet sins against Ophelia. Maybe you don't remember Hamlet's lines. I do. They stick in my mind. Hamlet says to Ophelia, "I did love you once." Ophelia answers, "Indeed, my lord, you made me believe so." Then Hamlet cuts her with the words, "You should not have believed me. I loved you not!"'"

Diane said, "I started reading the titles of the books on the pastor's shelves and understood why he could preach so elegantly. A whole row of Shakespeare. Milton's *Paradise Lost*, George Herbert's *The Temple*, Henry James's *The Golden Bowl*. And *The Pilgrim's Progress*. The classics.

"Walt, when I'd first come into this pastor's office I was ready for him. If he blamed me, or if I got a whiff of man-sweat, I was ready to jump up and flat walk away. But the man had read more than I had ever read. He fascinated me.

"He said, 'Last year I saw an extraordinary production of *Hamlet* in London. I had never seen what great actors can do. Even while Hamlet is berating Ophelia, the actress communicated the hurt and the grief his words were causing her. "Get thee to a nunnery!" the Hamlet-actor shouted. "Why wouldst thou be a breeder of sinners? Go thy ways. Get thee to a nunnery!"

"'Listen, Diane. It's the expression on Ophelia's face that has made me think of you.'"

Five o'clock. The sun broke through the rain clouds. There must be, I thought, a rainbow somewhere. The cooks had finished the evening meal. The waitstaff (as they were called in that progressive mountain village) were setting the tables. I was irritated by their clattering of plates and silverware. But Diane paid them no mind. She kept talking.

"That pastor took time to light his pipe. I think it was to allow me time to consider this 'Ophelia' thing.

"Then he said, 'You're hurt, Diane, the grief I see in you— well, I believe there's someone you haven't yet forgiven.'

"Cutting close to the bone, did I say? Well now he *hit* the bone. Yes, O Lord, yes. There were people I could not forgive.

"The pastor said, 'Let me tell you a little more about Ophelia. Even while Hamlet is still stomping around, Ophelia prays, "O, help him, you sweet heavens!" And she prays, "O heavenly powers restore him!" Diane, it seems to me that you haven't yet reached that part yet. Forgiveness.'

"'But,' I said, 'what if I *can't* forgive?'

"'You don't have to,' he said. And this, Walt, is how he set me free. He said, 'Forgiveness is a free gift, freely given. Its source is the crucified Lord Jesus. Listen, now. This is very important. If forgiveness is forced on you, if churches *demand* that you forgive someone, then it becomes a law that must be obeyed. It isn't freely given. You see? I don't doubt that the one who sinned against you needs forgiveness. But *he* is the one who disobeyed the laws of God. So, let *him* go straight to the source of grace. Let him go to the cross and fall down before it and confess his sin.'"

The waitstaff had turned on the dining room lights. The dinner bell rang. Diners were filing in, chatting, laughing, finding seats at the tables. And my friend Diane? Well, she had changed. Laughter twinkled in her eyes again.

She sat back and said, "Do you understand? It's not the *having to* that set me free. I'd been a pretty good teacher before. Now I was released to be a loving teacher too."

She leaned forward. "There's one more thing. The morning of the twenty-third of December—I will never forget the date—I woke up so lighthearted I was like a feather floating in the air. And I knew why. I had actually forgiven my family! Can that have happened in my sleep? Why not? Even *that* is a gift."

✦ ✦ ✦

How petty were the sins committed against me! Me, the aggressive and unforgiving King of the Road. Yet how greater was *my* sin. I lacked the grace of Jesus. Had I never taken to heart the call of Saint Paul?

> As God's chosen ones, holy and beloved, put on compassion and kindness and lowliness and meekness and patience, forbearing one another, and—if anyone has a complaint against another—forgiving each other. As the Lord has forgiven you, so you also must forgive. And above all these things, put on love, which binds everything together in harmony.

Consider Diane's story over and over again.
To the cross, Walt! Kneel down. Confess.

# CHAPTER 12

MARY: A HUG AS HOLY

AS THE OCEAN

Long ago, dear Mary, in the concourse of the San Francisco airport, I gave you so loud and harsh a scolding that travelers looked at us. This was Holy Week in the spring of 1987. You were my daughter, fourteen years old. I was your father, forty-three, berating you until, in that public place, you bowed your head. Your hair fell like a veil over your face. Though I couldn't see it, I heard it. You were crying.

✦ ✦ ✦

Grace Lutheran Church was small and inner city, yet we had developed a large choir of more than forty members. We named it "The Sounds of Grace." The choir consisted of youths, mostly, teenagers and college students. A number of adults would travel with us on our many tours, everywhere from Florida to Texas, through the whole Midwest as far as Colorado, New York, too, and Canada. And now, California.

The churches that accepted our requests to sing for them—well, I suppose they expected a handful of choristers whom they would encourage with smiles and soft applause. But the members of every church were astonished when the Sounds actually sang. We were that good. Our programs were dramatic, as if they were theater. Between one song and another I told stories. We might begin in the back of the sanctuary and sing ourselves forward. Or move into various groups. A soloist might surprise the congregation by singing from a balcony—that sort of thing.

Timmy Moore had a tenor voice so wide and comforting that he seemed to lift people on a cushion of song. Dee Dee Lawrence could rise through four octaves—a bird on the wing. And Gina Moore's soprano was a silver lariat.

We landed in the Los Angeles International airport on the Saturday before Palm Sunday. Our first concert would take place Sunday evening at a Lutheran African American church in Inglewood, but we had arrived early enough to worship with the congregation Sunday morning. Except for the white pastor, Jim Lobdell, the church's members were the same mix of colors as was the Sounds. Lurena and Michelle were glossy black panthers, Dee Dee and Timmy filbert-brown, and Tony feathers of a cowbird.

Reverend Lobdell began to preach in tones low and gentle. Minute by minute, however, his voice rose until it had taken on a nearly Baptist force. Gloria Ferguson, who was sitting beside me, said, "Ooo, he tingles me down to my toes."

Soon the people were calling, "Preach it!" and "Ay-*men*!" and "Hallelujah!" and Lobdell broke into outright singing. Before the end of the first verse, the whole church had joined him, clapping and rocking.

*Lean back*, the service proclaimed. *You're in for the duration.* The duration indeed. It lasted two hours, flaming with so genial a spirit that no one wished to be anywhere else. We sang with them heartily, and they with us.

The Inglewood Church became our home. The blood of the Lord kinned us into a single family. *Amen, preacher! Praise God! Hallelujah!*

✦ ✦ ✦

Monday morning the Sounds of Grace took to the road, a caravan of eight rented minivans following the coastal highway north, the blue Pacific to our left and sweeps of beauty rising from our right. Timmy Moore let out a low whistle.

Monday night, a concert in Oxnard. Tuesday morning, and we were driving along the hills. The shores of the sea were rimmed in petticoats of a slow foam. Shining black boulders bulged in the water. The heaving waves crashed against them, throwing up a jubilation of white clapping hands. And great crimson-colored cliffs rushed down like stallions galloping.

*How excellent is thy name, O Lord! How excellent is thy name!*

Three nights later in San Francisco, the Sounds of Grace sang its last concert.

"Have your bags packed by seven in the morning," I said to the forty voices. "We've got to return the minivans and be in the airport no later than eight-thirty."

✦ ✦ ✦

Mary, it was on the floor of the terminal that you dropped your airline ticket.

What has the power to annihilate the grandeur of the Creator in an instant? Great malevolence? Monstrous wickedness? No. Petty irritations. Minor fits of self-righteousness. Mere faithlessness.

I saw your ticket among the feet of the crowd. I didn't see you. And all the genial congregations in California were suddenly nothing. I saw red.

Well, Vicky Tyus had already lost her ticket. I'd spent time at the Delta counter proving that her name was on the manifest. Then there was a hubbub of teenagers gathered around the actor Danny Glover, begging for autographs—among whom was your own head of straw-blonde hair. I swam through the throng. There was your ticket like trash on the floor, but you had vanished. We had ten minutes before boarding, and I despaired. Dear God, I feared I was going to lose a daughter to California!

Finally you emerged from a restroom, pink-cheeked and cheerful—and I snapped at you. Heedless of people around lined up and walking down the concourse, I scolded you like an army sergeant with short, loud barks. You put your head down and began to cry. Even at fourteen years of age, Mary, your tears were so quick to come. I'm sorry. I am so sorry. I must have wiped out your Holy Week too. Pettiness can be so deadly.

But listen to the grace of God. Though sin may cancel the California coastline, yet forgiveness can restore it again. Forgiveness is nothing less than re-creation.

Once the airplane had leveled into its flight I sought you

out. I kneeled in the aisle beside your seat and confessed my sin. I had hurt you, and your tears were hurting me too.

But it was you who accomplished the healing. You turned and hugged me. O child of God!—you laid your cheek against mine, and the ocean rushed back into its place, and the week was holy again.

# PART 6

## CATCHING

## THIEVES

## CHAPTER 13

LUCIAN: OF PASTORS

AND THIEVES

The sewage system in the inner city surrounding Grace
Lutheran was hopelessly old. A spring rain would fill the
streets—Gum, Eliot, Lincoln, Garvin, Governor—with small
lakes. The church sat on a low hill which was, nonetheless, high
enough to save it from a forty-day-like flood.

It was May 1985, at eight o'clock in the evening, when a most
memorable thunderstorm hit with the suddenness of the hand
of God. The first rip of lightning occurred while I was teaching
an adult confirmation class in the basement of the church. The
windows flashed. Then came the boom of thunder, and then a
salvo of a hard rain. My class consisted of about eight adults. We
looked at one another.

"We gotta go!"

Outside, like strobe lights, the bedazzling lightning caught pictures that fixed in our eyes the rain and the new-forming lakes and the cars whose tires were already half under water.

Lucian Snaden was a tall, muscular young man. Most members of the confirmation class were able to start their cars and drive carefully through the flood, leaving V's in the lake behind them. One elderly woman could not walk through the water to her car door. Lucian and I pushed the vehicle to higher ground. Finally he and I were left standing alone under the roof of the church's porch. He was waiting for his mother. I was keeping him company. Between the bolts of lightning only the one bulb under the porch roof shed a sort of orange light.

On the other side of Grace Lutheran's building was a small brick house divided from the church's wall by a narrow sidewalk and a concrete porch. Several years ago the house had been a parsonage. Now it contained offices for my secretary and me, a kitchen, a workroom, and a room with shelves for all my books.

Last autumn and later in winter the church had been burgled. We'd lost our silver candlesticks and then the electric keyboard in the sanctuary, so we had moved all our valuables into that house of offices.

Lightning riddled the heavens. Out loud I counted the seconds. "One, two—" The thunder that followed could not have been more than two miles away.

Lucian and I were prepared to brave the waters whenever his mother drove into view. His face was composed. Neither the wind nor the weather troubled him. He was a man of silences. I commented on our rotten sewer system. He gazed into the rain and said nothing.

Suddenly, in the interval between thunder-crashes, I heard glass breaking behind the church. Lucian remained calm. But I dashed around the building. If a tree branch had smashed a window, then rainwater was blowing inside, destroying things.

But it wasn't a branch. It was a thief standing on the old parsonage porch! *He* it was who had broken the window! My blood shot to anger. The flat stupidity of the thing! Hadn't that thief seen the lights in the church windows? Couldn't he see that people were inside the basement?

I yelled, "Hey!"

The man yanked his arm from the broken glass and snapped upright.

Lightning flashed. He was a skinny little fellow, wide-eyed and frightened. His arm had been cut. It was bleeding. The advantage was mine!

"Look at me!" I cried. "I want to memorize your face!"

BOOM! The fellow's mouth was open on some vowel.

I leaped to the porch.

He whirled around and jumped off into the grass.

I ran after him, thrilled with the chase.

The grass was wet. His shoes slipped. He belly-flopped and went skidding through the water. He scrambled to his feet and kept running.

"Hey!" I cried again.

Lightning arced. Why, the man was just a *boy*! Wiry legs and terrified eyes, and I felt a personal power.

I tackled him. I pressed my right hand on his chest.

BOOM!

I raised my left arm and pointed to heaven.

"That," I shouted, "is for *you*! God is saying, 'Get away from my church and never come back again!'"

Lightning. His face was streaming water. His clothes were drenched and covered with mud. He was barefoot.

I thought I heard him whimper, "Please—"

BOOM!

"The voice of an angry God!"

He wriggled out from under me. I let him go and stood up. So much for robbers and thieves.

Then I, the Conquering Hero, strutted back to Lucian under the roof of the church porch.

"Know what I just did?" I said. I was a head shorter than Lucian, nor ever athletic. You can imagine the pride with which I told him everything that had happened, describing in detail my defeated adversary.

For the first time that evening, Lucian spoke. He said, "I know him."

"Know who?"

"That boy. His mama named him Centurion. We call him One Cent. Now his mama calls him Five Dollah, because he the onliest one left to look after her. They poor. Cain't buy medicines for her. She need her medicines."

The Reverend Pastor Walter Wangerin Jr. had been sure that *he* knew the boy. I hadn't known him at all. By my vaulted anger I had thought to exclude him from the church. Instead, I had excluded myself.

# CHAPTER 14

# MATTHEW: BECAUSE
# HE CRIED

Twice in time God established a covenant, a testament, with humankind. Twice he made a people to be his own. The first failed. The second is everlasting.

"You have seen what I did to the Egyptians," the Lord said to Israel, "how I bore you out of slavery on eagles' wings and how I brought you to myself. Now, therefore, if you will obey my voice and keep my commandments, you shall be my own possession among all peoples."

This first covenant was defined by God's laws. The benefits to Israel would have been incalculable: to be given their own land where flowed milk and honey; to become a great nation; to live with him, with the Lord God himself.

It was not for ignorance, then, that they broke the commandments, nor for want of trying, since they repented over and over again. Rather, "the imagination of the human heart is evil continually."

In the first covenant God's part was to offer blessings, and the people's part was to obey. On account of the failure of the people to uphold their part, it was the covenant itself that failed.

In the second covenant, therefore, God in Christ decided to take *both* parts upon himself.

Mercy hath a human face.

Jesus entered the sorry sphere of human affairs. He became flesh. With a perfect obedience he fulfilled not only the righteousness demanded by the first covenant, but also our ruination of that covenant, which demanded the sentence of death. He died. Was crucified and died, and we beheld his glory, glory as of the only Son from the Father. And from his fullness have we all received grace upon grace. "Jesus is Lord!"

There follows, then, this mystery and this miracle, for which Matthew is the evidence: *that we can be changed.*

✦ ✦ ✦

I suppose I could have accounted for my son's sins by arguing his natural exuberance. From the beginning Matthew had been an irrepressible child. Whims in him were deeds immediately. He didn't think. He acted. Did the boy want comic books? What else, then, but to go out and take them?

However I might account for it, Matthew stole, and I could not permit that. Stealing had a flat Old Testament law forbidding it. *Thou shalt not!*

And so it was late one night that I heard soft bumpings in the bedroom upstairs. The boy should have been asleep.

I climbed the stairs. Matthew was sitting on the bedroom floor, reading one comic book while others were scattered all around him.

"Matthew," I said, "where did you get these?"

On the top bunk Joseph, too, was awake, squirming on behalf of his younger brother, though that brother was quite free of guilt.

"From Heerdink," he said—the road we'd lived on before moving into the city.

"Heerdink? What? Were they just flying through the fields?"

"No."

"What then, Matthew? Where did you get them?"

"From the barn." One of our neighbors had a barn in which *his* son stored his comic books.

"Well, they're going right back. You will confess what you've stole! And you will return them. And you will pay twice what they are worth."

Again, Matthew had not the least tinge of guilt when he performed the law I'd set down before him. A sweet apology and easy recompense.

It must not have been more than a month when I stood praying a nighttime prayer with my boys.

> Jesus, Savior, wash away
> All the sins I've done today.
> Help me every day to be
> Good and gentle, more like thee—

"Matthew!"

The bottom drawer of his dresser was half open. That drawer was filled with stacks of comic books.

"Where did you get *these*?"

Brightly, guiltlessly, he said, "From the library."

Evansville's East Branch Library was just across the street from our house.

"You took them out?"

"Yeah," he said.

"Or did you just *take* them?"

"Yeah. That."

So I gave my son another, harsher commandment.

"Tomorrow," I said, "you will return every last comic book directly to Mrs. Outlaw."

I considered this to be a truly serious threat, for the librarian stood tall and strong and staunch. A magnificent and absolutely moral woman. Her spine was composed not of bone but of rectitude. Her eye could flash divine lightning. I'd seen smoke and fire issue from her nostrils. When tough young men parked their cars outside her library, drinking, smoking, and playing their radios so loud that their vehicles rocked with the rhythm, Mrs. Moses strode out and caused the men to tremble. They turned their ignitions and drove meekly away.

In the morning I walked into the library and said, "Have you noticed the loss of library comic books?"

Two tablets of stone doth Mrs. Outlaw carry when she crosses her arms beneath her breasts. She glared at me and said, "*All* the comic books."

"Well," I said. "Matthew is the culprit. I will send him in. Do whatever you want to do with him."

My heart shrank for my son. There he stood, his eyes barely higher than the great stack of comic books upon his arms, his Afro like a dark moon setting.

"Go," I said.

And Matthew went, a pipet climbing the broad stone steps of the brick building built by Andrew Carnegie.

I paced for more than fifteen minutes. Surely the fire on the holy mountain would be worth the refinement. Surely my Matthew's iniquity could not abide this Appearing.

The library door opened. My little boy came out with his explosion of hair and his eyes as wide as sunstroke.

As we walked back to the house I said, "Did Mrs. Outlaw have something to say to you?"

He nodded.

"Did you understand what she was saying?"

He nodded.

"Well, I have something to say to you too."

I spoke in detail about the consequences of sin. To me *steal* was a witching word of primordial power. Fully as much as I loved my son, I feared for him. *Perdition* had always been my mother's word when I was a child. It always caused my butt to tingle. It frightened me then. For the sake of my boy, it frightened me now. I warned him that one sin would lead to another. I had visions of Matthew sitting in some lockup somewhere.

"Do you understand?" I said, and he nodded.

Well, he might have understood, but he didn't change.

It was in the summer, ten months later, that I accepted an invitation to teach a seminar in St. Louis. The family went with me. We were loaned the use of an apartment.

At home again, I found—I don't remember *how* I found—another trove of comic books. These were perfectly new, each in a transparent slip-cover, and, so it seemed to me, unread.

Dear Jesus, the boy *had* to change! I *had* to impose upon him a law and a punishment as severe as the laws and the punishments that God had imposed upon his people, Israel.

There was no help for it but that I had to spank him.

"Matthew!"

"Yeah, Dad?"

"Go into my study and wait for me."

Wordlessly he went. I closed the door behind him and catechized myself. Nothing should be done in anger. But neither should I for pity foreshorten my arm. I would use my own hand in order to feel the pain that he would feel. And I would restrict myself to five swats exactly—not too few, or the medicine wouldn't take. Not too many, or I would raise in him an anger that would not soon be quenched.

I went into my study and closed the door. Matt was sitting on a straight-backed, dining table chair. I sat on another. "You," I said, "need to be spanked."

His head went down, his spirit drew away from me.

All over again I repeated the laws and their consequences. The possibility of hellfire at the end of an unrepented life. "Do you understand?"

He nodded. He always nodded.

"I'm going to spank you, Matthew, so that you won't suffer a punishment far worse than mine. Come here."

I had him lie belly-down across my thighs.

I raised my hand.

The instant I brought it down on his bottom, it stung, and my son stiffened as straight as a board. His affliction, my affliction. So then: two, three, four—Matthew did not cry. He refused.

Five.

I led him back to his chair and told him that I would leave him alone, that I would be back in a little while. I did not want to be the voyeur, who gets off on someone else's suffering. He should be allowed to cry in private.

Once outside of the study, I burst into tears. Oh, this was more than I could stand. I covered my face and sobbed loud enough that Thanne heard me.

"Wally?"

I fell on her neck sobbing, unable to say anything. I was so sorry, so frightened and sorry.

When I'd gotten control of myself again, I went into the bathroom and splashed cold water on my face. I dried it vigorously in a towel, then went back into my study.

Discipline must never end with pain. If I had touched my son to hurt him, now I touched him to love him.

And I said so. "I love you, Matthew. I will always love you."

I hugged him very, very tightly.

✦ ✦ ✦

Through the years that followed I came to believe that the Law and its Punishment had changed my Matthew. He did not steal.

Shortly before he entered his first semester of high school, Thanne drove him and Joseph, Mary and Talitha to the mall to buy school supplies. Back home again, she told me this story:

In the car the kids had begun to talk about things they'd done as children.

Talitha told her mother that she used to snitch cookies. Mary that she smeared her mouth with lipstick. Matthew that he used to sneak out of bed at night and slip into the kitchen, and make himself sugar sandwiches. Literally. He poured sugar on slices of bread and ate three or four sandwiches right heartily. Ho ho! A hyperactive boy, feeding his hyperactivity!

Then Matt turned to the topic of comic books.

Thanne said, "I was glad when you stopped stealing, or Dad might have gotten a bad reputation." She quoted Saint Paul. "A pastor has to be above reproach, managing his household well, keeping his children respectful in every way."

Matthew said, "You know why I stopped stealing?"

Thanne said, "Because Daddy spanked you."

"No, Mom," said our son. "Because he cried."

✦ ✦ ✦

Mercy hath a human face. It is not the administration of the Law. It is *mercy* that transfigures us.

# PART 7

# SERVING

# THE

# LEAST

# CHAPTER 15

# BILLY: THE RUINATION OF MY THANKSGIVING

Gloria Ferguson worked for the Salvation Army. In that capacity, she served the poor, giving them clothes: peacoats, warm boots in the winter, a warm shower and a cot at night, milk and hot meals, whether in the Salvation dining room or else by carrying them to the homes of the hungry.

Gloria telephoned me. "It's Billy," she said. "He needs a little help. Says he hasn't eaten for going on three days. It's Thanksgiving tomorrow, and I have my babies to tend to. Pastor, it'd be a load off if you'd take a bag of food over to his house."

"I can do that," I said.

"Billy's ninety-seven," Gloria said, "and a bit crotchety. Don't mind his wordy stab-sticks."

✦ ✦ ✦

As a shepherd separates his sheep from his goats, so did the King of Glory divide the nations gathered before him, the faithful to his right, the neglectful to his left. Even though the sheep didn't know him, they served him. Therefore, he invited these faithful into the kingdom prepared for them. To the goats on his left he said, "I was hungry and you gave me no food, thirsty and you gave me no drink, a stranger and you did not welcome me, naked and you did not clothe me, sick and imprisoned and you did not visit me."

And the neglectful answer, "Lord, when did we see you hungry or thirsty or a stranger or naked or sick and in prison, and we didn't serve you?"

"Truly," said King Jesus, "when you did not serve the least of these my brothers, even so you did not serve me."

✦ ✦ ✦

Billy's house was on Kentucky Avenue. When I arrived, I found the door standing open. The interior room was dark. I knocked on the doorpost. No one answered. I knocked again. Billy must, I thought, be home, or else he doesn't worry about thieves. My grocery bag was growing heavier by the minute. I knocked a third time, then turned to leave, but heard a high-pitched yell. "Whad-ya wait'n for? I'm hungry! Git on in here!" So I did. I entered.

The salt-stench of urine twisted my nose. Waves of roaches rushed from my feet. My eyes adjusted to the dark. Billy's ankles were sockless and spotted with dirt. His shoelaces were untied, his eyes bright, and crumbs were caught in a four-day's growth of whiskers. The old man crouched in an overstuffed chair like a buzzard.

I said, "I'm Pastor Wangerin. Gloria Ferguson told me that you haven't eaten in days."

Billy glowered at me.

I said, "If you want, I'll heat a bowl of chicken noodle soup."

Without shifting his eyes or his posture, Billy screeched, "Kitty kitty kitty!"

There came a crash in the kitchen.

Three cats streaked into the room, saw me, stiffened their legs, and slid to a stop.

Billy's bright eyes twinkled with hilarity. He cracked his ribs with laughter. "Eee, hee-hee-hee! Ain't lonely. Got me my zoo."

Here I was, a pastor well-dressed, clean and cleanly shaven, assaulted by his zoo of cats and ripples of roaches. My pride was piqued.

"Rest your coat," Billy screamed. "Set and talk awhile."

I kept my coat on. I didn't sit. There was nothing to talk about.

Billy kept his crouch, glaring at me, while his three cats menaced me by raising the fur on their backbones. I was beginning to regret my good deed.

Finally Billy shrieked, "Yer bag, boy. Carry it to the kitchen. I got some-pin to show ya."

At the word "kitchen," the cats turned tail and ran from the room.

The ninety-seven-year-old man had trouble getting out of his chair. In an effort to rise he leaned forward till his ears were between his knees. He rocked back, gripping the arms of his chair, then thrust himself forward again with a greater strength. Half-standing, he grabbed my suit jacket lest he drop to the floor.

"Cain't fall," he said. "Done fell too many times. Hurt m' spine, ya know. Got to rubber ma-self to standin'. Whad-ya say you did? Worked at?"

"Never mind," I said, yanking my jacket from his hand. I wanted to make haste to the kitchen and then be gone from this house.

Billy's kitchen! It overflowed with food! A canned ham on an ironing board; cereal boxes and boxes of macaroni-and-cheese and a bottle of vodka in his cupboard; the kitchen table stacked with unopened cans of pork-and-beans, tomato soup, Beefaroni.

He pushed food aside to make a space on his counter. "Here," he said. "Lay ma groceries here." He went to his ice-box and opened the door and peered inside. "Less see," he said. "Ain't got milk but what's gone sour. No butter. Cain't eat bread with no butter. Cain't eat Cap'n Crunch with no milk."

Billy turned to me and screamed, "Get me milk and butter and cream!"

I'd like to end this tale by saying that my service was rewarded. That Billy had, perhaps, given me a nickel, even a candy bar in return, but that would be a sentimental lie. There was no thanksgiving from Billy to me. Nor did I return to his house. No milk, no butter, and surely no cream.

✦ ✦ ✦

*Why do you serve me? Why do you allay my hunger with food?*

There is but one right answer.

"Because you asked me." That were enough to say. But better than that answer is this: "And because I love you."

# CHAPTER 16

‾○○○‾

# JUNIE PIPER: NONE
# SO PRECIOUS

The black telephone box was attached to the wall. No dial on its face. Simply, I lifted the receiver, put it to my ear, and waited while it rang upstairs. The desk sergeant behind me paid no attention. I was standing on the first floor of the county sheriff's building. I could hear the clattering of the typewriters beyond the sergeant, together with constant conversations, and now and then a bark of laughter. The second and third floors were jails for the county's prisoners.

"What?" said a voice on the other end of the line.

"Pastor Wangerin," I answered, "to see Junie Piper."

I was connected to one of the guards on the second floor.

"What do you want?" he said, as if I hadn't told him already.

"Mr. Wash Piper is a member of my church," I said. "I'd like to visit him."

The guard's mouthpiece was muffled—by the palm of his hand, no doubt—yet I could hear his call, "Wash Piper in here?"

Another, more distant voice, "Processed yesterday. Cell six, on three."

The guard picked up his receiver and said to me, "Stand by the elevator." *Click*, and the connection broke off.

This was the procedure. There were no buttons marked 2 or 3 to push. The elevator was controlled by the guard upstairs, according to his whim and in his own good time.

Nevertheless, I didn't have to wait long before the door slid open. The compartment smelled of stale cigarette smoke. Its walls were padded, and itself a claustrophobic cube. The doors slid shut. I'd put on my clerical collar in order to identify myself and my pastoral privilege. I carried a Bible and the small black box in which I kept the elements for communion.

I stepped out of the elevator into a cinder-block room. Fixed in the wall to my right were rows of small cubbies, each with a framed screen and a key to lock it. Close to the far left corner was a metal door, and directly opposite the elevator a thick window behind which sat the guard, a number of rifles on brackets on the back wall. The guard spoke through a hole in the glass.

"Empty your pockets," he said. "Coins, wallet, matches, a cigarette lighter if you have one. That wristwatch too. Store your stuff in one of those receptacles and give me the key."

"Can I keep my Bible?"

"What've you got in that little box?"

I opened it and showed him. He was doubtful about the small cruet of wine, but he nodded. "Fine," he said. Then, standing up, he said, "Tarry a quick minute, Reverend. I'll be right with you." He disappeared.

Shortly the metal door swung open. The guard put out his hand. "Peter Wagner." We shook hands.

"Walt Wangerin," I said. Then Peter said, "Do you think you can get Wash to talk?"

"Isn't that *your* duty?" I said. "Don't expect me to reveal what he tells me."

"Not what I mean," said Peter. "Wash hasn't spoken a word since he was arrested. He just lay down in his cell. I don't believe he's moved a muscle, neither last night nor today. Perhaps his pastor can snap him out of it. Come with me."

The guard's hard heel hit the floor with loud *clacks*. The keys that hung from his belt jingled. He led me down a long hallway, outside windows to our left, a series of barred cells to our right. Like the cells of a beehive, each of *these* cells duplicated the rest: eight feet deep and five feet wide. A metal bunk covered half the cell, a metal sink, and a steel, lidless toilet. Nothing was hidden.

Peter Wagner stopped at cell number 6. "Piper," he said. "Your pastor's here." Then he walked away—*clack clack* and *jingle jingle*—and left us alone.

Junie was lying belly-flat on the floor, his head on his forearms, his Afro flattened. He wore nothing but his undershorts.

I squatted down before the bars, wondering whether he would let me touch him. I decided that it was best not to.

"Junie," I said, "you remember me? I'm Pastor Wangerin. We've met often in your mama's house."

Junie Piper did not acknowledge me. He didn't so much as twitch.

Wash Piper: every time he passed through his mother's living room, she introduced me as if we'd never met before. In those days Wash had a velvet, midnight complexion and sorrel eyes as moist as a fawn's. Though he'd glance at me, he never smiled.

Now, here in his cell, Junie's complexion was ashen.

I said, "I'd like to talk with you. Do you mind?"

He gave no indication whether he minded or not, so I talked. This, that, and the other.

Junie Piper had just mustered out of the United States Navy. I think he might have been discharged for some infraction, because he came home beleaguered and lost.

I said, "What motivated you? I mean, why did you roll that old man right in front of the sheriff's office?"

I read the Twenty-Third Psalm aloud, trying to call Junie back into being. But it was as if there were no world around the boy, no universe, because he had become a nothing in a nowhere.

About fifteen minutes later I heard Wagner's heels and his keys.

"Afraid that your time is up," he said. Then he said, "Wash, at the least flush your toilet."

When I returned two days later I did touch him. I stroked the hair of the poor, debased young man.

"So," I said, "I hear that you were a cook at the naval base. And that you tried to get a job cooking for the restaurants here in town, even for McDonald's, I hear. I'm sorry that no one hired you."

I visited Junie twice the following week. It wasn't much of a breakthrough, but on my last visit he began to make a purring sound. I knew that he was eating better; I saw an empty food-tray on the floor. Moreover, he was lying on his bunk. Peter Wagner had let me enter Junie's cell.

I sat on the edge of the bunk and said, "Your mama doesn't come to church much. She tells me it's because she's lost her uppers. Did she, Junie? When I carry communion to her she gums the wafer." The first wonder that day: Junie shrugged his shoulders. Immediately I followed up with, "She hasn't lost her uppers, has she? I'll bet she eats corn on the cob, right?"

Then came the second wonder: Junie chuckled!

I jumped to my feet. "Peter!" I called. "Peter Wagner, can you hear me? Wash and I—we need a room to ourselves!" There were ears in every other cell. I wanted privacy.

Peter was indeed within earshot. His hard heels and his keys signaled his approach.

The third wonder: Junie Piper stood up.

We were led into a small room, the walls painted white. Two chairs inside, and a metal table between them, and a wire-mesh window in the door. Peter said, "I'll give you twenty minutes," then locked the door and walked away.

Junie and I sat facing each other across the table. I leaned forward, gazing at the possibilities in my bony black child.

"So, here's a story," I said. "There was a daddy who had a son. Now, that boy, he ran off with half of his father's money. Might have joined the navy, who knows?"

Junie's elbows were on the table, his cheekbones on his hands.

I said, "But money doesn't last. You know that. As long as

he had it, the boy had lots of friends. Parties, you know. Salted chips, reefers, booze, and all that. But when the money ran out, his friends took off, and the boy was left alone. What did he do then? Well, because he felt nothing but sadness, he went and robbed a man. I don't know, Junie. Maybe it was out of despair. Maybe it was just something to do, or else a crime to give his life a jolt."

I opened my Bible to Luke 15 and began to read the parable itself out loud. "There was a man who had two sons . . ." I verily believe that Wash Piper Junior was listening to me as he had never listened before.

To me it seemed no more than five minutes when I heard Peter Wagner's footsteps returning. I saw his face in the wire-mesh window, then he knuckle-rapped on the metal door. Oh, Junie! The knock had terrified him. He sprang up, throwing his chair backward. He slammed his hands against his ears. His eyes rolled exactly as a horse rolls its eyes when someone lashes it across its face. Junie swayed and started to fall. I jumped around the table and caught him and held him tightly. I wanted to *be* the world he seemed to have lost. I wanted my arms to be Junie's universe. I whispered in his ear, "I love you, Junie. And God loves you too."

How long thereafter? I scarcely remember. Two days? Three? My telephone rang. "Reverend Wangerin?" a woman said.

"Yes. That's me."

"Will you accept this call? I have to reverse the charges."

A long distance call then. Maybe a friend. Maybe even a member of my church.

"Of course," I said.

The operator said, "Go ahead, Mr. Piper. Your pastor's on the line."

I heard nothing but breathing.

"Hello?" I said. "Junie?"

More breathing.

"Junie!" My heart was beating as if in a panic. But it wasn't panic. It was anticipation. My precious, precious child. "Junie! Are you going to talk with me?"

A low voice said, "Well."

"Junie! Oh, Junie, I can't stand this. *Talk* to me!"

"Well," he said in a sweet, distant voice, "I love you."

And he hung up.

And I wept.

For Jesus has a velvet, midnight skin and great sorrel eyes as moist as a fawn's.

PART 8

DIVINE

INTERRUPTIONS

# CHAPTER 17

# MELVIN: HONOR
# THY MOTHER

I drove north on Interstate 94 from Valparaiso, Indiana, to Milwaukee, then took Interstate 43 north the twenty-five miles to little Cedarburg, finally turning onto the narrow county road to the dairy farm where Melvin lived. It was a bright October day. I hadn't seen my friend since long years back when I sat in church beside him for his father's funeral.

Mell and I had been roommates during our freshman year at Concordia College. Already then he showed himself to be a curious fellow. Many of the men in our class would slip off campus to drink beer. Nor did I refuse one or two myself. But Mell—he drank tea. He kept a small electric heater on the windowsill. He would heat a pot of water to a boil, dip a Lipton's teabag in and out of the water, then pour the light brown fluid into a cup, sit, and sip.

After that year Mell didn't return to school. It was in July that his father died. He stayed home to work the farm.

I had a deep affection for Mell's mother. When we were still freshmen, he would invite me to his home. Gertrude would spend Friday evenings baking a week's worth of bread. And pies. She earned a little extra money making and frosting wedding cakes. Gertrude was round and energetic with hands hardened by labor. Her face was as brown as the covering crust of an apple pie. She kept a large vegetable garden. Up before a Saturday morning I helped her load her pickings into the back of the station wagon. She drove the two of us to the farmer's market in Cedarburg, where we set out boxes of various vegetables and fruits and sold them to sharp-eyed German women.

"Kartoffeln. Wie viel?"

Potatoes. How much?

I would state the price.

"Nein!" a woman might answer. "Bringst du Frau Weiss."

Gertrude could haggle with the best of them. Often they paid her one or two dimes above the asking price.

I rapped on Mell's farmhouse door. It was painted white, almost blinding me in the October sunshine.

In a moment the door swung open.

"Why, Walter," he said. "What a surprise."

"Well," said I, "the notion struck me and I came."

"And I'm glad of it. Come in."

Mell wore a pressed white shirt and jeans with creases ironed down the pant legs.

I smelled new-baked bread.

"Your mother still keeps her custom, I see."

"No," Mell said. "These days I see to the necessary things."

✦ ✦ ✦

The commandments haven't expired. Nor have the holy promises been abolished. When I am asked regarding the future of human communities or whole countries or even the church on earth, I answer, "As long as people obey the fifth commandment."

Are there children singing songs for their ancient mothers? Have they never ceased to honor her even when she has become dishonorable in the eyes of others? Then I say, "The signs are good."

The best sign for the future of any community—whether it shall live long or short—is not financial, political, demographic, nor the size and the fight of its armies. The sign is moral. Don't measure the *strength* of a nation. Rather, assess how its people *behave*.

Moses in Deuteronomy 30 says, "I have set before you life and death, blessing and curse. Therefore, choose life." If we walk in the ways of the sustaining God and obey his commandments, then we have chosen life, for the Lord *is* life.

When the parents who have raised us harden into crankiness, what then? When their bodies become as light as will-o'-the-wisps, and they have ceased to tell you that they love you, what then?

"Honor" in Hebrew is *kabod*. Honoring our parents, then, means to grant them the weight of authority and the heaviness of a long life's wisdom. This, writes Saint Paul, is the one commandment that comes with a promise.

Honor your father and your mother that it may be well with you, and you may live long on the earth.

Here the Hebrew word for "earth" embraces three meanings: long on the *land*, on your fields, your farmlands and on the fruit of your labors; and *land*, the territory of your country; and *land*, a long life on this globe, the earth.

And so we—so long as we sing to the mother who bore us the songs of her childhood—we may live long on the land and on the land and on the land.

✦ ✦ ✦

"I see to the necessary things," Mell said to me. He ducked his head in something like an apology. "Mother can't," he said. "Come with me, Walter. Greet her."

He led me into the parlor just off the kitchen. There was a sideboard against the nearest wall, an easy chair in a corner, and beside that a small table on which were books and needles to knit and the yarn for knitting. A shaded standing lamp was bent over the back of the chair. Across the room was a hospital bed cranked up to allow Mell's mother to sit.

Gertrude was not what I remembered. Her round face had the glaze of an empty dinner plate. Her watery eyes never reached mine but dribbled down to my hands.

"Mother," Mell said, "be pleased to welcome my friend, Walter Wangerin."

I reached to shake her powder-white hand and closed, it seemed to me, on soft dough. I stepped back. "Mother thinks you brought food." Mell went to a bowl on the side table and brought forth a prune. Gertrude still had a set of strong teeth. She was munching happily when we left the parlor.

For the rest of the afternoon Mell and I strolled through an apple orchard. The chilly air smelled of dry things, husks and hulls and autumn leaves. Apples were rotting on the ground, touching the air with a winey aroma. Mell said that he was laying money aside for a nursing home, should he die before his mother. It was he, now, who carried vegetables to the farmer's market, and apples, when they were in season, and strawberries and raspberries and plums. He earned money by baking wedding cakes and knitting—scarves, sweaters, blankets, baby buntings.

At dusk we returned to the house. Mell scrambled eggs. We drank several bottles of beer, then stood up. "Goodnight," he said and went into the parlor to read and to sit with his mother. I climbed the stairs and slept in the bedroom we had shared when we were young.

I have always enjoyed my friend's probing intellect, his soft-spoken conversation. He was a wise man. He could counsel senators and CEOs, would they have listened.

At three a.m. I was startled awake by a yowling cry. I thought it was a cat, a lingering, inarticulate feline lamentation: "Yah, nah-nah, nah, nah, YAH!"

No. It wasn't a cat's wail. Too human for that. Something was wrong.

I ran downstairs. No lights in the kitchen—only a weak strip of light through a crack in the parlor door. I pushed it open, then stopped. The source of the light was Mell's standing lamp. Mell himself was kneeling beside the hospital bed. A brief moment passed, and then the odor in the room told me what my friend was doing. He was washing Gertrude's waste away. He was changing her diapers. He was honoring his mother.

Mell turned and saw me in the doorway. He smiled and motioned me to his chair.

And he was doing something else. Melvin was singing to her:

> "Müde bin ich, geh zur Ruh,
> Schliesse meine Aeuglein zu . . ."

A lullaby. The simple, sacred, nighttime, and everlasting song.

And this is what Gertrude was doing. She was singing with him. Not a lamentation, neither hurt nor sorrow, but an old woman singing with an outrageous pleasure at the top of her lungs.

"Yah, nah-nah, nah, nah, *YAH!*"

And lo: Gertrude's face was alive again! She was the little girl who first had heard this lullaby, innocent, happy, and wholly consoled. Ah, young Gertie—dressed in her Easter best and ribbons in her hair—was running the green fields, her arms spread, all good things coming to her. And the last good thing was that her parlor door was open to the Kingdom of Heaven.

✦ ✦ ✦

Ask me about the future of human communities upon earth, whether their lives shall be long or short, and I will answer, "Listen to that boisterous singer. Watch the gentle ministrations of her son.

"Yes," I will say, "the signs are very good."

# CHAPTER 18

# JOSEPH: A SUPERNAL PARENT'S DIVINE INTERRUPTIONS

The Lord, the Lord," said YAHWEH to Moses while that prophet was on Mount Sinai. "The Lord, a God merciful and gracious, slow to anger and abounding in steadfast love and faithfulness, forgiving the iniquities of the parents upon the children and the children's children to the third and the fourth generations."

I have collated two texts into one, both from Exodus 34. Nevertheless, this is the gist of God's proclamation. Something wonderful has been passed down from Israel's ancestors, and from our ancestors to us.

In Jeremiah 31 the Lord says: "But I shall watch over them— the Children of Israel—to build and to plant. In those days they shall no longer say,

> The parents have eaten sour grapes,
> and the children's teeth are set on edge.

"But"—and here comes a harsher word—"but those who die shall die for their *own* sins. Those who eat sour grapes, *their* teeth shall be set on edge."

It may be a harsh word, yet it implies this goodness: that my sin need not be passed down to my son. In that sense, he is free of me.

On the other hand, there is the similarity that we might bodily *look* the same.

O Joseph, beware what you mock in me, for soon it will be yourself whom you are mocking.

✦ ✦ ✦

My poor son. Today he is an adult with an aggressive schnoz on him. A dorsal fin. A battleax with which to cut the air. A nose of royal proportions.

From Joseph's birth the Creator had given the mostly gentle child an artistic aptitude. Already by the time he was three years old, Joseph was drawing tiny little stick figures.

Once he sat between the back of an easy chair and the wall behind it. When his mother started to vacuum the living room, she pulled the easy chair away from the wall and saw an odd sight. She thought the chair had left a shadow on the wall paint in the perfect shape of the back of that chair. But a closer inspection revealed what that shadow was: the pencil drawings of a hundred tiny stick figures, each with its own face, each with its own mood, no two figures were alike.

Once upon a time when I was driving Joseph eastward along

a country road, and the sun was sailing behind us, Joseph was kneeling on the back seat, looking out the car's rear window.

Suddenly he said, "Look, Daddy! The sun's following us in an Indian boat!"

I looked at the sky in my rearview mirror. A cigar-shaped cloud was eclipsing the bottom half of the sun—or *I* would have said it was a cigar. Joseph, on the other hand, saw a canoe. An artistic aptitude had he, and an artistic eye.

In grade school the kid drew caricatures. One of these depicted his teacher with a wicked precision, catching some quirk of hers and exaggerating it. Straightway his classmates knew whom he had drawn. Though he was shy and quiet, Joseph had a crack-shot sense of humor. He had turned the teacher's bottom lip into a rubber blob so funny that even she laughed.

Inside his mind Joe saw the world as weird. God might repent of having given the kid the artistic gift, since it could create weapons. But the gift was Joseph's now. If he wished, he could caricature even the Lord God himself.

Now, I tell you all that to tell you this.

Thanne and I had decided to teach our children about sex as they approached puberty one by one. The boys were mine to teach. The girls were hers.

So it came to pass in the autumn of 1982 that I drove my twelve-year-old boy from Evansville into Kentucky, from our house to a cabin on Lake Beshear for three days of sex instruction. The woods on the far side of the lake seemed to be on fire—reds and yellows, furious oranges and umbers as dark as sleep. The autumn winds blew the leaves from the trees, leaves looking like nothing so much as a woman's long hair streaming in the sky.

We spent Friday evening talking of nothing important, eating, playing Monopoly, and finally going to sleep. I had decided to save the more difficult conversation until tomorrow afternoon. You know: sex, how babies are made, physical maturity, genuine love, and so on and so forth.

We rented an outboard motorboat. Joseph hopped in beside me. What speed! We left a sweeping wake behind us. We investigated small islands. I used to smoke a pipe in those days. I was clenching it now between my teeth, hands on the steering wheel, crouching forward, somewhat tense, hoping we wouldn't run out of gas before getting back to the cabin again. Were there oars in the boat? Yes. Oars.

That afternoon I took Joseph on a walk and spoke my speech. He was mostly quiet. Bemused, I think. When I was finished, Joe told me that his fourth-grade teacher—a weaselly fellow who wore brightly patterned bellbottom pants—had pretty much sickened him on the idea of begetting kids by sex. Too physical. Too messy. Joe figured that adoption would be better than the strange engagement of bodily parts. Maybe he intended to set me straight about baby-making and maturity and genuine love, and so forth.

Joseph! Convinced he could make adult decisions from the get-go.

And Joseph the talented.

Saturday evening he put his sketch book and pencils on the floor, lay down on his belly, and drew a cartoon.

I'm afraid to say it, but it was of me.

There I was in profile, gripping the wheel of the speedboat, gritting a long-stemmed pipe between my teeth, smoke boiling out the bowl of that pipe—and, plowing the air in front of my face, a nose as big as a moldboard! A tractor, nostrils flaring, forehead swept back, and an eye both bright and tiny and intense.

Poor Joseph.

The caricature was both accurate and hilarious. That single explosive nose *forward-ho!*-ing across the lake . . .

But now my boy is himself an adult with two boys of his own. And that riotous caricature of our noses? His too.

✦ ✦ ✦

I am your father, Joseph Andrew, with all my sins and iniquities. But God is your *supernal* parent. Because of *his* son's wounds and because of his divine intrusions into our lives, the deep furnace of my angers has not been handed down to you. True, you might have gotten my hypersensitivities and something of my lifelong melancholia—for which I do honestly apologize. But you have *not* gotten my peevish irritabilities. You are more gentle with your children than I was with mine. You are kind, and so much more willing to sacrifice yourself than I have been, sacrificing even the time you might have devoted to your art, to your designs, and to your adept, well-crafted sculptures—images in clay, you see, of the images in your mind.

God is your father. God is my father too. In spite of my destructive disobedience, he bequeaths to me the humility, the manner, and the love of his son, Jesus. These are our legacies, Joe, yours and mine. Grace has made it so. And in your face I have seen it so.

Ever and ever, praise to our Father! And unto you, my son, my heartfelt gratitude forever.

PART 9

AN

INVASION

BY GOD

# CHAPTER 19

◦◦◦

# AGNES BRILL:

# ALLERGIC TO GOD

Walter Martin Albert Wangerin (my father's name, not mine) was a pianist of many parts. I mean that he could be as sober playing Bach and slap-happy playing honky-tonk and boogie-woogie or soulful playing "Beautiful Savior."

Once Walt Sr. sold our only car in order to buy a baby grand piano, which was given pride of place in the living room. In bed at night I would hear him playing for himself alone. He played in the dark—improvisations on the theme of a German hymn, or a deep-thumping and tweedling jazz. Whether he was melancholy or contented, I could always measure my father's mood.

Sometimes Walt Sr. would crouch over the piano keys in Immanuel Lutheran Church's fellowship hall. He'd turn his head, look slyly at the youth-group behind him, pull a long face, and say, "Don't laugh. This is a sad, sad song," and then he would sing:

> Go tell Aunt Rhody,
> Go tell Aunt Rhody,
> Go tell Aunt Rhody,
> Her old grey goose is dead.

> We must have a fun'ral,
> We must have a fun'ral,
> We must have a fun'ral,
> They knocked it in its head.

I can't have been more than six years old, and my brother Paul five, when Dad began to teach us how to play the piano. We learned middle C and its scale; learned "Chopsticks"; learned to finger the theme from Hayden's Surprise Symphony.

> Papa Hayden, dead and gone,
> But his mem'ry lingers on;
> He played *[something]* tunes like this,
> *Dah-dah, dah-dah, dah, BOOM!*

It wasn't long before Reverend Wangerin gave up teaching his boys. But our mother never wavered. *Her* boys were *going* to be taught, even if it was the last thing she did.

Therefore, I was eleven and Paul ten when Virginia introduced us to our new piano teacher, an old, sad Teutonic man who smoked incessantly. The cigarette smoke-stink in his living room caused us to blink back tears. The flats of this man's fingers were as wide as spatulas, and their skin was stained brown with nicotine. Sometimes, when our teacher meant to show us how a particular piece should be played, he would close his eyes, rock backward, lose himself in the music, and take a marvelous flight to God knows where.

Ten dollars a lesson. Twenty for the both of us. Twice I lost a twenty-dollar bill, whether going to our lessons or coming home, I didn't know. Virginia sent me out to search the sidewalks over and over again. But lost was lost. I never did find her forty.

I can't remember, now, when or why we left that sad piano teacher. This I do remember, that when I was a freshman in college I taught myself to play the first flourishes of Rachmaninoff's Second Piano Concerto, just those few bars and no more. Mother said, "See? You *can* play." Well, no, I couldn't. I was faking it.

After that a thousand pursuits—at which I was a thousand times more successful—buried the piano.

✦ ✦ ✦

Well, the eldest Wangerin boy grew into a man of thirty-two years, and, like his father, he became a pastor, though his congregation was small, inner-city, and African American.

By then Thanne and I had come into possession of a blond upright piano. Once more it occurred to me that I might take another run at learning how to play it. Since the instrument was terribly out of tune, I asked a young friend to come and see what he could do for it.

Brian was a lanky, fawn-eyed fellow, so unassuming that he talked softly, scarcely moving his lips. He brought to our house a small wrench, but no tuning fork since he was endowed with perfect pitch.

I sat and watched Brian tap-tapping a key while working a

little wrench. When he was satisfied with the sound, he moved to the next key. My friend's patience taught me patience.

Finally Brian played chords up and down the register. He stood up and said, "You're good to go."

I said, "Can you recommend a piano teacher? I'm afraid I'll have to start at zero."

"Well," he said, "there's Miss Agnes Brill. She's taking on new students."

"Miss Brill," I said.

He looked at me doubtfully, then said, "I don't know."

"Right," I said. "Too old to start."

"It's not you," he said. Then: "I guess a pastor knows how to deal with troubled people."

He told me that he knew the woman well. He visited her every Sunday. They would sit at the piano and play side by side, after which she'd cook roast beef and gravy, carrots and mashed potatoes. Then they'd sit and eat and talk until the food had grown cold.

"She's a bit excitable," Brian said. "She hates waste. And I think I should tell you, well, Miss Brill has allergies."

✦ ✦ ✦

Agnes Brill's ancestors were Cornish. Her complexion was pale, the skin across the bridge of her nose so tight it was white. Likewise, the clothes she wore were linen, white, undyed. The woman's hair blow-away soft, her wrists thin. Like a bird's were the bones on the backs of her hands, her fingers spidery, and her expression brittle. I put her around fifty years old.

My first lesson lasted no longer than ten minutes. Miss Brill positioned herself on a small stool some little distance from my right elbow.

"Show me," she said.

I glanced up. What was I supposed to show her?

She gestured toward the keys. "What do you know? What can you do?"

I ran a clumsy scale in C major.

She said, "D minor."

I scarcely remembered where to place my hands, let alone play the scale.

"Get up," she said.

I did.

She said, "Stand back." She lifted the top of the piano bench and took out a beginner's book: the elements of fingering, staffs, major and minor chords, scales, and so forth. She flipped to the back of the book where there were simple, five-finger exercises. "This one," she said, "and this one. Learn them before your next lesson."

I did that too.

The following Thursday I played the pieces for her. I might, or I might not, have met her expectations. As long as I continued my lessons, my teacher never praised me or condemned me. What was, was.

Once, in the chill of mid-October, Miss Brill ended a lesson by playing Chopin, a nocturne. So melancholy was the music, so light and tender were my teacher's fingers on the keys, so sadly and quietly did she bring the piece to its close, that I too was moved to sadness. I was surprised, then, by her harsh accusation: "You're wearing wool!"

In fact, my shirt was cotton, as were my blue jeans.

"Your socks," she said.

I rolled up my pant-cuffs. Indeed—the socks were woolen.

"I'm allergic to wool," she said. "It's the animal lanolin."

"But—" I didn't believe her.

Early in November I arrived wearing a paisley rayon scarf.

Miss Brill snapped, "Take that thing outside."

I said, "It isn't wool."

"Do you think I exaggerate?"

"Well—"

She grabbed the scarf and ran it over her arm. Almost immediately the skin puffed up in an angry red welt.

Her allergies were intensifying. Animal lanolin had been bad enough, but now she'd become allergic to synthetic fabrics and color dyes.

We met on Thursdays. Come Thanksgiving I planned to spend the holiday with my family. Apparently Miss Brill did not want to break our regular schedule. Lessons were more important than *anyone's* family. As for me, the family took precedence. The Thursday after Thanksgiving, my teacher declared that I had defied her. She sat on her stool without another word.

Soon the woman was stuffing lengths of white linen under her front door and along the sills of her windows. She was convinced that the wind blew allergens into her house.

Yet, when she played the slow movement of a Scarlatti sonata, I could sympathize with her. She gave to human loneliness a universal name. She consecrated the human condition, and I felt that I could understand her.

Miss Brill's next effort saddened me. She began to fight the very atmosphere itself by hanging white sheets over her every interior door and by covering the carpets with sheets. I played the piano in a ghost's abode.

Then came the Thursday when I began to question her sanity. She met me at the door, taut and panicking. "There's a mouse in my kitchen. Get it out!"

All this happened exactly as I am telling it to you.

The kitchen was polished to a shine. Nothing was out of place. The baseboards were solid—no holes, no mouse. I turned and found the woman right behind me.

She said, "It's in the refrigerator."

I opened the refrigerator door.

"In the vegetable drawer."

This was almost more than I could take.

Finally, the last time I visited Miss Brill I canceled our lessons and ended our relationship altogether.

It had snowed. White outside, white inside. The woman was sitting and staring out a window, erect, stick-thin, and desolated.

"Miss Brill?"

"Another allergy," she whispered. "I don't know what to do."

Nor was there anything that I could do.

"Myself," she murmured. "I'm allergic to my own body."

✦ ✦ ✦

April, it must have been. Or May. On a breezy springtime afternoon I met Miss Brill as she was coming down the steps of the city library. The air was scented with a vernal loam. The woman wore a light leather jacket. I greeted her and told her how glad I was for her recovery.

"No thanks to you," she said. "To Brian alone." She passed me by and went on her way.

When later I had the chance, I asked Brian what he'd done to help Miss Brill.

The lanky fellow shrugged. "Not much," he said.

"But something," I said. "She praised you."

"Well," he said, "I visited her. I played piano with her. I ate her Sunday meals."

He said he'd done no more than that. In fact, he had done *much* more.

As always after they'd finished eating, the two talked, or simply sat in silence.

"Waste not, want not," Miss Brill would say, then give Brian a clean spoon and place the boat of cold, clotted gravy before him. My friend would not deny her, but would eat the gravy gone.

✦ ✦ ✦

Humanity's profoundest allergy is to be afflicted by one's very self. All must endure it. Sin pervades us through and through.

# CHAPTER 20

# JOSEPH: THE KID WHO WAS THE JUDGMENT OF GOD

During the early 1980s I tended to come home for supper in a foul mood.

Congregations pay their pastors to be good. Me. I was *very* good. I visited the sick, the shut-ins and those in jail. I confronted the city administration on my congregation's behalf. I counseled couples preparing to marry and arbitrated between couples preparing to divorce. With a pastor named Loomis Dillard, I created an inner-city improvement agency. On my own I established the Mission of Grace, which served the poor in every respect. I baptized, I confirmed, I presided at funerals, I preached acceptable sermons.

So good was this minister, in fact, that he would spend twelve hours a day away from home.

Consequently, I forgot about my daughter's birthday.

Thanne scolded me. "Not even a card!"

Twelve hours, I say. I was growing weary of well-doing. Though I hid my exhaustion from the congregation, I took it out on my family.

✦ ✦ ✦

When the prophet Jeremiah became depressed by his God-demanded mission, he prayed an angry prayer. "Thy words were found," he said, "and I ate them. I did not sit in the company of merrymakers, nor did I rejoice. Your hand was upon me. You filled me with indignation, and I sat alone." No parties for Jeremiah. No smiles on his weather-beaten face. Outrage, rather, at the children of Israel because they were stiff-necked, hardhearted, and bull-headed. Furthermore, Jezebel, the wife of King Ahab, was seeking to kill him. "Why is my pain unceasing?" Jeremiah complained. "Why is my wound incurable, refusing to be healed?"

Not only was the prophet weary of well-doing. He was downright bitter. He hurled an accusation into the face of God: "Wilt thou be to me like a deceitful brook? Like waters that fail?"

Having traveled more than halfway through the wilderness to accomplish his purpose, and trusting that the Lord would show him water in time to quench a killing thirst, Jeremiah fulminated against the deceitful Lord because when he arrived at the brook it was dry and the streambed had cracked under the burning sun. The prophet had gone too far to turn back, and yet was not anywhere close to the place where he was to fulfill his mission. What then? Did the Lord God mean to kill him?

But God answered his prayer—with judgment and with a

command. "If you return to me," said the Lord, "I will restore you. And if you utter what is precious and not what is worthless, you shall be as my mouth."

+ + +

In those days Grace Church paid me the meager salary of eight thousand dollars, scarcely enough to support my family. I was working twice the hours of a fulltime pastor but was being paid for no more than halftime.

It can be understood, then, why, coming home through a slushy January snow, I came home in a most foul mood.

We sat down for supper. I sat at the head of the table. Talitha sat around the corner to my right, and Joseph around the corner to my left. I can't remember what we ate. Vegetables from my garden, no doubt. Eggs from my chickens. Thanne's frugality balanced our poverty. For example, she would wrap the children's sandwiches in the wax paper she'd saved from cereal boxes. Before we began to eat, I demanded an absolute silence.

"Fold your hands," I said. "Bow your heads." We prayed our regular pre-dinner prayer: "Come, Lord Jesus, be our guest, and let these gifts to us be blessed."

Midway through the meal, Talitha began to fidget.

"Be quiet," I said.

I believe that she tried to obey, but fidgets became squirms, and squirms became whines.

"Talitha! I am *not* in the mood!"

Good mood or bad mood, it didn't matter. The headstrong girl got up, went to the cupboard, and brought back a box of crackers and a jar of strawberry jam. She thumped her butt on her chair and began to slather the jam on the crackers. In the process, Talitha let drop a dollop of the sticky jam on the floor. I decided that she'd done it on purpose. This was more than I could endure. With my forefinger I flicked the back of her hand, and she began to cry.

"I didn't hurt you!"

This did no more than to increase her crying. I pinched my lips and glowered at her. I was ready to retreat to my study. But son Joseph halted me.

The boy tilted his chair back on two legs. He looked at the ceiling and said, "Sometimes Daddy spanks us and we don't mind. It doesn't hurt. We laugh and have fun, because it's a birthday spanking and he's counting the years since we were born. He says, 'A pinch to grow an inch.'"

Joseph was the shortest boy in his school. He liked this "pinch to grow an inch."

"But when Daddy is angry," Joseph continued, "even a little flick hurts."

The boy brought his chair down on all four legs and started to eat again. It was as if he had commented on the weather.

But the comment shamed me. When I tucked Talitha in bed that night, I apologized abjectly.

Joseph was just a kid! Yet that kid had been the judgment of God.

*If you return to me, I will restore you. If you utter what is precious and not what is worthless, you shall be my mouth again.*

# PART 10

# THE
# UNINVITED
# GUEST

# CHAPTER 21

# MARY: "IT'S ONLY A DOLL IN THE BOX"

We had a custom at Grace Church. We would gather always on the Sunday evening before Christmas and then, bundled and hatted and happy, would sally forth into the sharp December darkness and sing carols to the shut-ins of our congregation. The children bounded ahead, squealing, excited by the thought of surprising them with song. The adults would walk behind, chatting, making congenial noises, puffing ghosts of breath beneath the streetlights, glad of the company.

"Think it'll snow?"

"Cold enough."

"Me, I'm smellin' a weatherly nip."

On this particular Sunday evening the stars were crystals in the heavens.

So we crowded Miz Moody's front porch.

*Hark! The herald angels sing glory to the newborn King . . .*

The porch light flicked on, a curtain opened, and there sat the white-haired Miz Moody, smiling through her parlor window and nodding to our rhythm. The children fairly burst with glee. *Go tell it on the mountain, over the hills and everywhere . . .*

We did silly things, like jangling our keys to "Jingle Bells." Even the adults were children, the white faces among us pinched pink, the black faces frosted as though the cold were a white dusting of snow.

Then down the street again, regaling Miz Buckman, Miz Lander, Mr. J. D. Jones. Timmy Moore sang "O Holy Night" in a generous tenor voice. "It is the night of the dear Savior's birth," and Timmy was the chariot that bore us up. Miz De Witt bowed her head and wept. His youthful voice had a locomotive power, singing truth, singing conviction. "O night! O night divine." We could scarcely breathe.

Then we all sang "Silent Night."

On the third verse Dee Dee Lawrence—that blinking, innocent, milk-chocolate dumpling of a child—took a descant flight. She soared like a meadowlark, straight up to the sparkling sphere of heaven. She touched it with her wing and all the round sky rang.

This too was our custom: to divide into three groups, each group to visit those members of Grace who lay in one of the city's hospitals.

On that Sunday evening, the twentieth of December 1981, Mary was seven and Dee Dee Lawrence eight years old. They were in the group I drove to St. Mary's Hospital, as were Herman Thomas and my wife, Ruthanne Wangerin.

I led them into Miz Odessa Williams's room. The children had never laid eyes on her before. Her body frightened them. They surrounded her bed on three sides, carefully touching nothing, for she was gaunt and cadaverous, her fingers pencil-thin, and her arms mere bones. I stood on the window side of her bed. Mary stood across from me. My daughter was speechless. Her blue eyes were growing large. Odessa was dying of cancer.

✦ ✦ ✦

Odessa had been housebound for the previous seven years. During all that time I had visited her once a week. She'd been a strapping tall woman of strong opinions and stronger affections. Our children's choir, *her* children's choir, was called "The Grace Notes." The woman had kept abreast of them by means of other visitors, by the telephone gossip system, by bulletins and newsletters—and by me. She pumped me for information regarding her "chirren."

Waving her old black arms, puffing an endless chain of cigarettes, striding back and forth in crush-backed slippers, Miz Williams would scold me if she thought I wasn't doing right by the children but would sometimes muse about her own born daughters who had passed away and left her to her own devices.

I learned to check her mouth when I entered her apartment. If her dentures were in, she was mad at me. She wanted her words to clack like weapons and to hiss with a precision equal to her anger. But if she met me with toothless gums, I knew that I had her approval. She would swell with a grand, maternal love for the chirren, even though she'd never heard them sing.

I was never able to persuade the woman to stop smoking. It was lung cancer, finally, that laid her on a bed in St. Mary's Hospital.

✦ ✦ ✦

Miz Williams's eyes were sunken in their sockets. Her flesh was as dry as parchment. Her big hands crossed themselves on the sheet over her caved-in stomach. Who could tell whether she was breathing or not?

Mary seemed unable to tear her eyes from Odessa's face. Every child was fixed in a terrible awe.

I said, "Sing, why don't you?"

But they merely shuffled their feet.

"What's the matter? Cat caught your tongues?"

Mary said, "She won't hear us."

"Well, solve that," I said. "Sing the same as you always do."

It was a pitiful "Away in a Manger." They were like nursery children uncertain of their audience. But then they found some comfort in the sound of their own singing, and they began to relax, and the carol strengthened.

And Miz Odessa opened her eyes. She began to pick out the faces of individual singers. Mary returned her look with a fleeting smile. So then the little choir were angels, joyful and triumphant! Odessa began to nod and to frown and to chew a fierce pleasure as if it were a delicious piece of meat. Now all the children found a first noel. They knew instinctively what the frown of an old black woman meant.

Odessa did not have her dentures in.

I whispered, "Dee Dee." She glanced at me. I said. "Dee Dee, 'Silent Night.'"

Dear Dee Dee Lawrence! That child, as soft as the shadows through the windowpanes, soared. The rest of the Grace Notes let her take the words while they hummed and harmonized along with her, all unconsciously. "Round yon Virgin, mother and child . . ."

Odessa's eyes widened. She found Dee Dee at the foot of her bed. And then, a marvel. She raised her long, long arms. Still lying on her back she began to direct the child. By strong strokes she lifted Dee Dee. She pointed the way, and Dee Dee trusted her. She sang a soprano descant higher and braver than she'd ever sung before. She became a fountain of light, and stroke by stroke, with her imperious arms, Miz Williams sent Dee Dee on a celestial journey to glory. So bright, so holy and high, "Christ the Savior is born! Christ the Savior is born." Dee Dee ascended as if the roof had opened to the night sky, and the stars themselves rang like bells in heaven.

Then the old woman brought the child by meek degrees down to earth again. "Jesus, Lord, at thy birth."

The Notes stood in silence, waiting for something.

Nor did Odessa disappoint them.

"Oh, chirren, you my choir," she said, catching each of them on the barbs of her words. "Ain' no one stan' afore you for goodness, no. Babies, you the bes' ever was."

The children gazed at her, believing her completely. My Mary, too, believed the woman, heart and soul.

"Listen me," Odessa said. "When you sing, wherever you go to sing, look on down to the firs' row o' chairs. Alluz one chair empty. See it?" The children nodded. They saw it. "Know what that chair is for? For me. 'Cause me, I alluz been wif you. Gon'

be wif you forever. An' you know how I can say such a macku-
lous thing?" They waited to know. "Why, 'cause we be in Jesus."
Odessa lifted her arm and opened her hand. "Babies, babies,
we in the han' o' Jesus—old ones, young ones, girl ones an' boy
ones, an' me an' you. An' no one gon' snatch us out. Jesus, he
don' never let one of us go. Never. Not never."

Mary reached out her own hand and touched Odessa's. The
old woman had won her heart. For this is the power of a wise
love wisely given: to transfigure a soul suddenly and forever.

✦ ✦ ✦

On Tuesday the twenty-first of December Odessa Williams
passed away.

Her death had been a long time coming, but quick when it
came. She went to God without her dentures.

*Quick when it came.* Odessa left us little time to prepare her
funeral. Gaines Funeral Home embalmed her body already
Thursday morning so that her wake could take place that same
evening, and we scheduled the funeral for Friday morning at
eleven o'clock. Friday would also be Christmas Eve. The mortuary closed on holidays—Holy Days. Also, Gaines never worked
on weekends.

Suddenly my pastoral duties were doubled and tripled. I
had to prepare a devotion for Thursday's wake and a sermon
for Friday's funeral. The children's pageant was to be presented
that Friday evening, Christmas Eve. Christmas Day required its
own sermon, as did the next day, Sunday. When I came home
for lunch Wednesday at noon, I was, therefore, distracted by my
hectic duties, was much less a father than a pastor.

While we ate grilled cheese sandwiches I mentioned that Miz Williams had died yesterday. The deaths of the elderly wasn't an unusual piece of news. But this death was *Odessa's*.

Mary put her sandwich down and stared at it.

I finished my coffee, wiped my mouth, and stood to leave. Then Mary said softly, "Dad?"

It was one-thirty! I said, "What? I've got to go."

"Dad?"

"Mary! What?"

"Is it going to snow?"

"Tomorrow? Before the wake?"

"Friday."

"I don't know. I'm not a weatherman."

In a tiny voice my daughter said, "I want to go to the funeral."

"Ask your mother!"

✦ ✦ ✦

Christmas Eve dawned grey and hard and cold and windless, clouds covering the earth. I walked to church.

We had a custom at Grace. An hour before a memorial service the casket was set and opened on a low table directly in front of the chancel. Relatives and friends, colleagues and acquaintances, those who could not stay for the funeral, came to church for a last viewing. This morning it was only a handful of church members. It seemed that no one had thought of Odessa but these few. By ten forty-five some of the mourners began to sit down in the pews. They kept their coats on. When a row of people had filled a pew, they made me think of birds on telephone wires, puffing their plumage against the cold.

I robed myself. This too was a custom of mine, to meet the family outside the door as they arrived in the mortuary limousines. But, as I said, this was Odessa Williams's funeral. She had no family. Then it was Mary standing before me on the church porch.

She pointed at the sky. As if it were an accusation, she said, "It's going to snow!"

Yes, the day was bleak. It looked likely to snow.

I said, "Come in while Mom parks the car."

Inside I led her up the stairs into the sanctuary. It was very small. Nine pews on one side of its single aisle, and eleven pews on the other. I led her up that aisle to Miz Williams's casket. My seven-year-old daughter looked down and murmured, "Oh, no. Oh, no."

Odessa's eyelids seemed to have been closed with glue. Her lips were too pale, and her complexion another color not her own—a false, woody brown. Perched on the bridge of her nose was a pair of glasses set askew. Glasses? If she'd worn them before I hadn't noticed it. Someone else had set them on her face.

After a hesitation Mary put out her hand and touched Odessa's pencil-long fingers. Immediately she snatched her hand back as if the fingers were a burring ice.

"Dad!" said Mary, glowering. "Miz Odessa is already cold! You *can't* bury her, because she'll be *covered* with snow!" Then she hid her face in my robe and began to cry, and I became a father again. My daughter had just touched death. The end of things. The knowledge that things *must* have an end. That Odessa Williams, that fierce old woman who had taken possession of Mary's heart only four days ago, that *she* had an end, has ended, is gone, is dead.

I knelt down and hugged Mary very tight until her sobs were stilled, then released her and watched her walk down the aisle like a poker soldier. She found her mother and sat. No crying anymore. Her lips were pinched into a knot. I noticed that other members of the Grace Notes had also arrived.

And so the funeral. And so the sermon.

But what to Mary were all the sustaining truths of Christendom? What was heaven? Nothing, because Miz Williams had come to nothingness.

Later, in Oak Hill Cemetery, Grace Church stood around the coffin in their heavy coats, and I read of dust and ashes, my words producing clouds of ghosts.

"Since Almighty God has called our sister from this life to himself, we commit her body to the earth . . ."

When we turned from the grave and began to walk to our cars I tried to take Mary's hand, but she refused me. She stumped to a stop. "Dad!" Her blue eyes were flashing. She pointed to the sky, then pointed to the ground. "See?" she demanded.

A fine, white powder was beginning to collect at the bases of the headstones. In heaven the powder was darker. It was snowing.

✦ ✦ ✦

Daughter Mary had been chosen to play the role of the Virgin Mary in the pageant that same evening. I thought that this might be too much for her.

She was lying face down on her bed when I entered her bedroom.

"Mary?" I said.

She didn't answer. Her small form tugged at my heart. I said, "Should we get another Mary tonight?"

She said, "I'm Mary."

"Oh, I know that. What I mean—another girl to *play* Mary."

She repeated, "*I* am Mary." Mary she was. Mary she would be.

Friday evening, then, Grace congregation found Christmas greens hanging from nails on the sanctuary walls, and a Christmas tree decorated with paper sheep and donkeys and little mangers, handmade and child-made, hard to recognize except for the bold printing, "I AM A LAMB." The sanctuary lights had been dimmed. Only in the chancel were they bright.

Little shepherds in bathrobes and little angels in white gowns marched up the aisle. A decree went out. The giggling play-actors lined up on the chancel steps and belted out "Angels We Have Heard on High." A bearded Isaiah jumped into the pulpit and shouted, "Fear not! Good tidings of great joy!"

Thanne and I were sitting among the members of the congregation, the second pew from the front.

The shepherds and the angels began to sing "Away in a Manger" while three small figures moved up the aisle, Mary (the child and the Virgin) carrying a floppy brown doll, Joseph (a boy named David) holding up a great big hammer, and Laurie, a sort of innkeeper/stage manager carrying a wooden crib filled with straw. Laurie placed the crib in the center of the chancel floor. David went around and stood behind it, facing the congregation. And Mary knelt. It was without tenderness that she dropped the doll on the straw.

So now the shepherds who had been watching their flocks by night crowded behind Joseph and kneeled in a gaping adoration.

Suddenly all the angels were waving wands with folded aluminum stars stuck to the ends of them. And little Isaiah was God, bellowing, "All right!"

And all the children brought joy to the world because the Lord had come.

But Mary? She began to enact a scene of which Saint Luke knew nothing at all.

She picked up the raggedy doll by its kinky hair. She stood. She gathered up the skirt of her virgin-blue dress, and stepped right over the manger, and walked out of the chancel into the darkness of my small vestry at its side.

Well, the children lost a little of that joy to the world but doggedly sang on. Some of the adults around Thanne and me began to crane their necks. "What's the matter with that one?"

For my own part, my heart melted to water within my chest. The day had been altogether too much for my child. I thought I should get up and follow her, but Thanne touched the back of my hand and shook her head.

Just as angels and shepherds were wondering at Jesus's love, Mary returned without the doll but with a genuinely joyful smile. Briskly she clipped it back to the manger and knelt down and placed the doll gently in its manger, and put her palms together like the first Mary after all, and beamed a nearly blinding radiance.

Then all the lights were extinguished and, while burning candles were passed along the pews, everyone began to sing "Silent Night," and Dee Dee Lawrence—well, she took wing and climbed so high that women wiped their eyes with the tips of their hankies.

+ + +

After the pageant, Thanne drove our other three children home. Mary chose to ride with me. A sifting snow made cones below the streetlights. It swirled on the road before us and blew lightly across the windshield, closing us in a cotton privacy.

I drove awhile in silence.

Then Mary said, "Daddy?"

"Yes?"

She said, "Jesus wasn't in the manger. That wasn't Jesus. That was just the doll that Rosaline owns.

"Daddy?"

"Mary?"

"Jesus doesn't *have* to be in a manger. I mean, he can go back and forth. Up and down. One time in heaven, another time on the earth, right?"

"Right," I whispered.

"So his manger is empty! The same with Miz Odessa. I figured it out. We don't have to worry about the snow because it's only a doll in her box. If Jesus can cross this way to that, so did Miz Williams cross."

*Jesus, he don' never let one of us go. Not never.*

Then Mary turned and looked at me. She said, "Why are you crying?"

# CHAPTER 22

# TALITHA: THE CALLER

Uninvited. Unappreciated. Feared, if she were known to be there, comes a guest to every happy gathering.

She cannot be controlled. It is she who controls. She is not kind. She does as she pleases. Therefore, if she *could* be known, the happy gatherers would make a pretense of not knowing. And this is a marvelous thing, that they would succeed! Though she moves ever among them, breathing down their necks, they dance their perfervid dances, by the motion alone denying her presence—until she touches one of them, and he stumbles, and he drops. And then the dance is done, and the dancers turn to mourning. And none can refuse her. No, not one.

Her name is . . .

✦ ✦ ✦

For her sixteenth birthday Talitha decided to give herself a surprise birthday party. My daughter—I guess she got tired of waiting.

Talitha is the youngest of our four children, adopted by her mother and me, just as we had adopted her brother Matthew three years earlier. Her birthday is on the ninth of January.

Thanne said, "I'll help you."

Talitha sighed and said, "I can handle it." Of course. That girl could handle anything.

Thanne said, "At least let's work on the guest list together."

"The what?"

"The guest list. The invitations. I'll save you time by writing the cards myself."

Talitha rolled her eyes. I could have predicted that. A parent gets only so much credit per month per teenager, and Thanne had used up all her credit over the Christmas season. She'd have to earn more before this child was ready to admit the authority or the wisdom of her mother.

"Won't be no guest list," Talitha said. "You just put out the word. *It's party in Talitha's basement, Saturday night*, and they come. *Who* comes is the surprise."

Thanne said, "What if strangers come?"

"There's no one I don't know."

"What about liquor? Liquor is strictly forbidden in this house."

"There's nothing we can't handle, Kenya and me." Kenya is Talitha's closest girlfriend. "Relax, Mom. We can handle anything."

I believed it. Our daughter is as bold and as self-assured as they come.

That is how Thanne had spent her credit.

After a night out, we, her bland parents, returned to find

Talitha sweating in the kitchen. She was rolling out the most enormous hunk of dough I'd ever seen in my life. It drooped over the edge of the kitchen counter.

Thanne asked, "What are you making?"

The girl said, "Coffeecake."

Thanne chuckled at such a foolish notion. She said, "Oh, Talitha! That's *four* coffeecakes." And there went half her credit.

Talitha stiffened over her blob of dough which was as huge as a bean-bag chair. "The recipe says *one* cake."

She (*I can handle it*) covered her monster with butter and sugar and cinnamon. She brought its ends around into the shape of a human hug, removed all the grates from the oven except the bottom grate, heaved the coffeecake in, turned the heat on low, then kept checking it with a toothpick until it had baked for, what? An hour and a half? Oh, more than that.

And it worked. And Thanne had lost the rest of her credit.

That is to say, Talitha's coffeecake had baked through and through. Its top glistered with a fawn-colored sweetness—and *then* she cut it into three parts. With one she fed the school marching band. One she allowed her family to eat. And the third she froze for her birthday party.

She and Kenya began to prepare the basement. A table for refreshments, paper ribbon streamers, my record player, and blacklight bulbs in the ceiling fixtures.

"Won't that make things a little too dark?" said I.

And she said, "No."

And she was right.

I should not have been surprised by the effect. When friends started to arrive, their eyes shined with a blue-white luster. So did their teeth. They wore sleeves which the blacklights turned bright as they began to dance.

Partway into the evening, three boys and a girl rang the front doorbell, none of whom I'd met before. They filed passed me, saying with dead faces, "Bosse, Bosse, Bosse," and "Bosse." Talitha's high school. Not waiting to receive my greeting, they marched downstairs.

Within two minutes they were marching—they were *being* marched—upstairs again, dead-faced still, but with Talitha and Kenya right behind like prison guards. "Don't come back till you come back sober!"

Big-bottle Cherry Cokes and 7Ups and Dr Peppers; pizza, chips, dip—and that coffeecake. And how the children danced! I found myself tapping my foot, moved by their beauty. They floated to the rhythms of the music. They didn't dance in pairs. They shuffled their feet and leaped all as a single body, and landed, and slid the floor, complex and confident and cool. It was a communal thing.

"*Boom*—I got your girlfriend! *Boom*—I got your boyfriend!"

Thanne came downstairs. Under the music she said to me, "You have a telephone call. I think you should take it."

The uninvited guest.

Thanne has an accurate instinct. On Saturday nights (except this Saturday night) I didn't want interruptions since I would be working my sermon for Sunday. She knew that. She wouldn't have brought this call to my attention if she hadn't thought that it was important. She said, "It's a woman. She said she lives in Iowa."

The floor upstairs trembled to the music downstairs.

I put the phone receiver to my ear.

"Hello?"

The woman's voice said, "Um."

"Hello? This is Pastor Wangerin."

The voice said, "Yes. Well . . ." Then, as if it were a race, the woman dashed through her next words. "I-just-wanted-to-say-goodbye-to-somebody-that-is-kind." She paused.

I said, "Do I know you? What do you mean, you're saying 'goodbye'?"

There was a long pause. The voice sounded like that of a younger woman. In her twenties? Her early thirties?

She said, "But I know you. I've read your books. You are kind."

"Really," I said, "I think that's beside the point. You must have some other reason for calling me long distance."

She blurted, "I can't take this anymore." Her voice fluted high. "I'm tired, Pastor. I am so . . . damn . . . tired."

There was no mistaking that her very life was failing. Suddenly her "goodbye" scared me.

"Listen," I said. "What's your name?"

"No. No need for my name."

Just then I heard an inarticulate whining in the background. The phone thunked on something hard. A table top? The woman's voice was distant now. She said, "Go back to bed. Leave Mommy alone." More whining. *"Go!"*

She picked up the receiver. "I love them," she said. "But I'm *bad* for them. I make them so unhappy. Better that they should have a different mother."

"Are you talking about your children?"

"I can't cook, I can't wash their clothes, can't wipe their noses. Oh, God, I can't do anything but sit and cry."

"Give me your telephone number," I said. I begged. "Tell me your address in Iowa."

*Boom—I got your girlfriend! Boom—I got your boyfriend!*

Soft laughter on the other end of the line. "No. I'm not in Iowa. I'm hiding my tracks."

"But you have to talk to someone."

"I'm talking to you."

"I mean someone face-to-face. Right now! At least tell me your city. I know preachers in every city. Let me call one for you."

"I am so tired," she sighed. Her voice diminished almost to nothing. "So tired. So damn tired."

"Please," I said. "I won't sleep tonight. It scares me to think that your babies will wake up tomorrow and find their mother dead. Please—"

She hung up.

I stood in my study still holding the phone to my ear, paralyzed.

The children dancing in the basement below me did not know, could not know, that the stranger-guest was among them, breathing down their necks, the terrible guest whose name is Death.

I was choked with pity for my daughter. Beautiful were her friends, dancing their arabesques. But their beauty, their dance, their strength, their happy confidence, and their sweet communion were so fragile. One day, one day they would all be dead and nothing of this mortal life would be left for them.

I sat down on the basement steps and mourned for their brazen fellowship.

*I can handle anything.*

No, not everything.

The telephone rang again. This time I didn't wait for Thanne. I rushed upstairs and caught it on the third ring.

"Hello! Hello—?"

"When I die—"

Yes! The same woman!

"When I die," she said, "am I going to go to hell?"

"What is your name?"

"I don't want to go to hell."

"I know, I know. No one wants to go to hell."

"But if I live"—her voice was urgent—"I'm worried they'll take my babies away."

A dilemma, yes. But *this* was a good dilemma! The woman was thinking of life, if not of her life, then of the lives of her children.

"Listen," I said. "Get a pencil. I want to give you my address." Drawers, then. The sound of a drawer being pulled open. "Do you have the pencil?"

"Um."

"Take this down." Number by number and word by word I spoke the address slowly.

"Now," I said, "do this for me. Just this one little thing. When you get up in the morning, write me a note. You don't have to give me your name. Write this: *Dear Walt, I woke up.* That's all. Just that. Will you do that?"

She said, "Elisabeth Anderson," and the line went dead.

I leaned my hands on my desk and dropped my head.

"Jesus. Oh, Jesus."

Thanne was standing beside me. "Wally?"

I couldn't move.

*Death, where is your sting? The sting of death is sin, and the power of sin is the law. But thanks be to God, who gives us the victory through our Lord Jesus Christ.*

"Just so," Thanne said.

That night it was my wife who became my Evangelist. Thanne pierced this poor pastor with the sacred spikes of truth and of life and of resurrection. And the handle of the hammer was in the hand of the merciful Son of God.

# WALT AT SEVENTY-THREE

So, then, with this final chapter my little book is finished.

Know ye that when an author writes, *what* he writes can talk back to him, revealing truths he'd known before but had not known that he had known. The sentences whisper, "Look and see. For the mind of Christ has always resided in *your* mind, patiently waiting to be heard."

The author's writing is like the hook that catches fishes. And every fish he lands tilts its bottle-cap eye to him and pops its cartilage mouth, calling the writer to humility and obedience of Jesus. To Jesus, the servant of households and peoples and nations and every human that populates the earth.